Finding God in the Dark

Finding God in the Dark

David Walls

VICTOR BOOKS

A DIVISION OF SCRIPTURE PRESS PUBLICATIONS INC.
USA CANADA ENGLAND

Scripture quotations are from *New American Standard Bible,* © the Lockman Foundation 1960, 1962, 1963, 1968, 1971, 1972, 1973, 1975, 1977. Other quotations are from *The Living Bible* (TLB), © 1971, Tyndale House Publishers, Wheaton, IL 60189. Used by permission; the *Holy Bible, New International Version*® (NIV). Copyright © 1973, 1978, 1984 by International Bible Society. Used by permission of Zondervan Publishing House. All rights reserved; J.B. Phillips: *The New Testament in Modern English,* Revised Edition (PH), © 1958, 1960, 1972, permission of Macmillan Publishing Co. and Collins Publishers; *The New Testament in the Language of the People* (WMS) by Charles B. Williams. © 1966 by Edith S. Williams. Used by permission of Moody Press, Moody Bible Institute of Chicago; the *International Children's Bible, New Century Version* (NCV), copyright © 1986, 1988 by Word Publishing, Dallas, Texas 75039. Used by permission.

Copyediting: Carole Streeter, Barbara Williams
Cover Design: Scott Rattray
Cover Photo: Stock Imagery

Library of Congress Cataloging-in-Publication Data

Walls, David R.
    Finding God in the dark / David Walls.
        p.   cm.
    ISBN 1-56476-132-0
    1. Suffering — Religious aspects — Christianity. 2. Consolaton.
    3. Walls, David R. I. Title.
    BT732.7.W35   1993
    248.8'6 — dc20   92-46501
                                                                                    CIP

---

1   2   3   4   5   6   7   8   9   10   Printing/Year   97   96   95   94   93

Contents

When the streams of life flow quietly and softly, it's not hard to find friends. But when those quiet streams turn into torrents of trouble, some of our "friends" can't bale out soon enough. So I am especially grateful to a handful of people who did not bale out on me, but chose to weather the storm by my side. With respect, admiration, and a heart of love, I dedicate this book to:

—**Bill and Frank Eubanks,** faithful friends and loyal co-workers, whose integrity and enthusiasm for the Lord stand as markers for my life. I continue to marvel at your faithfulness.

—**Vern and Jayne Giesbrecht,** whose enduring friendship through the last thirteen years has proved to be a source of stability and encouragement for me. As fellow laborers for Christ, your steadiness in ministry has often challenged me.

—**Lee Wiggins,** a young man who has always impressed me with his maturity and hunger for God and who serves with me now so effectively. May your zeal never be dampened.

—**Doug and Linda Klein,** whose enthusiasm, joy, and sensitivity will never be forgotten.

—**Brad and Patti Thiss,** who through the darkness of

their own lives have modelled courage and trust in our wonderful Lord.

— **Charlie and Becki Brueggeman,** who were always quietly available, always ready to stand tall when the winds howled the loudest.

— **Mark and Debbie Hardin,** who suffered when we suffered and who rejoiced when we rejoiced.

— **Karsten and Louise Solheim,** who have never stopped believing in me and who continue to this moment reaching out in generous love to my family.

Space does not allow me to list other special friends who rode the white water with me. I trust that you know who you are. The prayer of my heart is that each of you, whether written on these pages, or on the pages of my heart, will realize the tremendous positive influence you have had and continue to have in my life. Beside each of your names belongs one word: Irreplaceable. Thank you for all you mean to me. Thank you for helping me find my way through some of the darkest days of my life. I shall be eternally grateful!

David R. Walls
March 1993
Amherst, Ohio

Foreword

"Before God can greatly use a man, he has to greatly hurt him." I don't know who first said it, but I do know that I have tried to dance around it for most of my ministerial life. Hurt? Who needs it? Who wants it! Not me!

In fact, I clearly remember praying one day, "God please make me an exception. Please use me, but don't hurt me!" I doubt if God listened to that prayer. I am sure He did not honor my request. Looking back from this vantage point, I am thankful for the pain that God allowed in my life. I can see now that it has been productive. Somewhere in my barrel of sermons, I have a message entitled, "The Advantage of Adversity." Every once in a while, I pull it out, dust it off, and remember the week of anguish in which it was shaped.

I told some friends during those particularly difficult days that everyone experiences trouble. The difference is this: Some talk about it, others don't!

I am grateful that my friend, David Walls, has chosen to talk about his trouble. A book on *Finding God in the Dark,* would not interest me if I thought that the author had spent all his days in the sunlight. Because he shares his own personal struggles, I want to hear what he says!

Years ago, I heard Warren Wiersbe give a talk to pastors

entitled, "Send Us a Pastor Who Reads." Everytime I run across that tape, I think of David Walls. Everything that he writes and every sermon that he preaches is packed full of information that he has gleaned from his extensive research. He carefully connects the Eternal Word with current human problems and because of that, people want to hear what he says and read what he writes.

I was with David during some of the experiences he tells about in this book. I remember very vividly his anguish. He has not created this for effect. These things did happen to him. I also recall him processing these events and seeking to learn from them. Believe me, the wisdom in this book was gathered under extreme pressure!

A long time ago, I heard a preacher say that when God has you in His vice, you can kick and scream all you want, but He will not let you free until he has finished what He is doing in your life.

David Walls has spent some time in God's vice! Now he tells us what he has learned. You owe it to yourself to read what he has written. It's a lot easier finding God in the dark if you're following a good guide!

David Jeremiah
San Diego, California
March 1993

Maybe I was born out of time. I don't know. It's just that "The Andy Griffith Show" remains one of my all-time favorites. I even love to watch the reruns a second and third time. Usually I find myself laughing, but every once in a while, a line drops out of the dialogue that seems to have been written not for then, but for now . . . for me. There is one conversation that seems to apply particularly to this book. Barney, Andy's deputy, asks Andy how one acquires good judgment. Andy says he guesses it comes from experience. Barney asks how you get experience. Andy replies, "You get kicked around a little bit."

I would have to say that I too have been kicked around a bit . . . by events, circumstances, and people. And since the last eighteen years of my life have been spent in pastoral ministry, the great majority of that pain found its context within the church, among Christians. Hard to figure? We'll see as we get further into the book.

But let me say this. There have been times in my life when the pain seemed to mock everything I said I believed, when my insides hurt so much that I found myself in the depths of despair and wondered if I would ever be able to get out, let alone keep on going.

I remember with exacting detail a period of six years

when I wrestled with the pain of my only brother's sub-
stance abuse, to the point that I would get up at 2 or 3 A.M.
and drive through the streets of our city hoping to spot him
and bring him home. In the midst of that was the horrifying
reality that my parents' marriage was disintegrating before
my eyes and there was nothing I could do about it. Within
months of that, our pain was interrupted by the joy that
came from the birth of our first son, now fourteen years old.
Yet even through the joy, fear stalked us as Jeremy was
almost lost in the delivery room. Just weeks after his beginning gasps of life took on regularity and we smiled, my
wife's youngest brother, Bruce, age fifteen, died of a brain
tumor. Bruce, my friend . . . a kid who loved Jesus Christ
and people . . . was, in the month of his death, supposed to
head out as a short-term missionary for Child Evangelism
Fellowship. How could he be gone? That question haunted
me for a long time, especially when I glanced at a picture
we had of our Jeremy in the arms of his uncle Bruce.
Jeremy doesn't remember, but I do, and the pain shouts
again.

There have been other encounters with this monster we
call pain. Those I have just reviewed fall under the banner,
perhaps, of *personal* pain. Another kind would be that
which I would label *ministry* pain. This is more difficult to
write about, because ministry is my life. But there is no
question that this is where the pain intensifies.

Along with many others in ministry, I have found that
criticism seems to follow me like an unhappy shadow.
Sometimes it's more visible than at other times, but it is
always there, lurking, leering, laughing. And that keeps the
embers of pain glowing, threatening to burst into full flame
at any moment. But beyond that, I remember not so long
ago, in another city, another state, and another church. . . . I
remember with horrifying anguish, several years of pain . . .
knifelike and sinister in quality. I suppose the words ha-
rassment and character assassination would best fit those
days. Wave after wave of enemy artillery bombarded my

life. Our home was burglarized twice, the tires on our two vehicles were ice-picked late one night in a targeted attack, according to the police report. Our phone rang with so many lethal messages that the police tapped the line in an attempt to track those who rained their terror upon us. The police urged us not to allow our children to be out of our sight for fear for their safety. To make it all the worse, the lay leaders in this particular ministry seemed bent on my destruction, accusing me of most anything they could sink their teeth into. I was mercilessly lied about, told I was in need of psychiatric care, that I was not capable or deserving of the title of pastor; and then that same group even verbally flogged me in the presence of the congregation. It came to the point that I ended up in the hospital . . . chest pains shouting the pain of stress.

Now please understand what I'm saying here. This book is not about dysfunctional pasts. Neither is it intended to be an exposé of those who have come against me. I'm not into either. I'm into recovery. I'm galvanized by hope, not despair. So, this book is simply an attempt to wrap our security around the truths of the Scripture. . . . truths we must believe when everything is coming apart. The above slices of my personal library of pain are included only so that you realize that these chapters do not arise out of a vacuum . . . that they don't float mysteriously out of the fog of tranquility. Like many of you, I can identify with Anne Murray's plaintive lyrics:

> No, I don't think time
> is going to heal this broken heart.
> No, I don't see how it can
> if it's broken all apart.
> A million miracles
> could never stop the pain
> or put all the pieces together again.[1]

The good news is that adversity has a great deal to do

with our spiritual development. You see, when you get
kicked around a bit, it either knocks you out or you become
a better person. This book is an attempt to help us become
better people. The heart of it is beautifully expressed in the
words of the poet. Read them with your heart and put the
pain away . . . just for a moment . . .

> I will praise You, Lord,
> for You have saved me from my enemies.
> You refuse to let them triumph over me.
> O Lord my God, I pleaded with You,
> and You gave me my health again.
> You brought me back from the brink of the grave,
> from death itself, and here I am alive!
> Oh, sing to Him you saints of His;
> give thanks to His holy name.
> (Psalm 30:1-4, TLB)

*Beloved, do not be surprised at the fiery ordeal
among you, which comes upon you for your
testing, as though some strange thing were
happening to you; but to the degree that
you share the sufferings of Christ, keep on
rejoicing; so that also at the revelation of His
glory, you may rejoice with exultation.
If you are reviled for the name of Christ,
you are blessed, because the Spirit of glory
and of God rests upon you.*

*By no means let any of you suffer as a murderer,
or thief, or evildoer, or a troublesome meddler;
but if anyone suffers as a Christian,
let him not feel ashamed, but in that
name let him glorify God.*

*For it is time for judgment to begin with the
household of God; and if it begins with us first,
what will be the outcome for those who do
not obey the gospel of God? And if it is with
difficulty that the righteous is saved, what will
become of the godless man and the sinner?
Therefore, let those also who suffer according
to the will of God entrust their souls to a
faithful Creator in doing what is right.*

1 Peter 4:12-19

1
Surprised by Suffering

It happens every once in a while. When it does, you don't often talk about it except to yourself. It happens on those rare occasions when your day has finally quit throbbing and you are running pretty close to empty. It happens when you find yourself alone. . . . It's late and everybody else is counting sheep or dreaming dreams, but you're not. You're wide awake and reviewing the videocassette of your life, which you've just rewound. And you're wondering why things don't seem to fit together like they used to. You're wondering why you can't seem to keep the old ball of yarn from unraveling. You're wondering why it's happening to you. The more you rewind the tape, the more distorted the picture is and your night is still long.

In his book, *In the Eye of the Storm,* our friend Max Lucado offers this insight into your night. See if he's watching the same tape you are.

There is a window in your heart through which you can see God. Once upon a time that window was clear. Your view of God was crisp. You could see God as vividly as you could see a gentle valley or hillside. The glass was clean, the pane unbroken.

You knew God. You knew how He worked. You

knew what He wanted you to do. No surprises. Nothing unexpected. You knew that God has a will, and you continually discovered what it was.

Then suddenly, the window cracked. A pebble broke the window. A pebble of pain. Perhaps the stone struck when you were a child and a parent left home—forever. Maybe the rock hit in adolescence when your heart was broken. Maybe you made it into adulthood before the window cracked. But then the pebble came. . . . Whatever the pebble's form, the result was the same—a shattered window. The pebble missiled into the pane and shattered it. The crash echoed down the halls of your heart. Cracks shot out from the point of impact, creating a spider web of fragmented pieces.

And suddenly God was not so easy to see. The view that had been so crisp had changed. You turned to see God, and His figure was distorted. It was hard to see Him through the pain. It was hard to see Him through the fragments of hurt.

You were puzzled. God wouldn't allow something like this to happen, would He? Tragedy and travesty weren't on the agenda of the (God) you had seen, were they? Had you been fooled? Had you been blind?

The moment the pebble struck, the glass became a reference point for you. From then on, there was life before the pain and life after the pain. Before your pain, the view was clear; God seemed so near. After your pain, well, He was harder to see. He seemed a bit distant. Your pain distorted the view—not eclipsed it but distorted it.

Maybe these words don't describe your situation. There are some people who never have to redefine or refocus their view of God. Most of us do.[1]

REFOCUSING ON GOD

The Apostle Peter had to. More than once, it seems. The difference is that Peter wrote about it. Drawing from his own experiences with pain — experiences we bury deep down in our heart of hearts — Peter dropped a bucket into his heart and poured the contents out on the pages of the first New Testament letter that bears his name. We call it 1 Peter. It's really a letter about rocks, starting with the rock man himself, Peter. It's a letter about stones, about pebbles of pain that crack the windows of our lives. It contains some of the most vivid expressions of Christian hope and courage through suffering that you will find any-where in the New Testament. In fact, Peter mentions *suf-fering* some sixteen times and uses eight different Greek words to make his point. He etches these words onto the chalkboard of our lives in order to strengthen us, to encour-age us, and to remind us of something we'd prefer to forget.

> Beloved, do not be surprised at the fiery ordeal among you, which comes upon you for your testing, as though some strange thing were happening to you (1 Peter 4:12).

The words *fiery ordeal* quite literally say, "the painful trial that burns in your lives." For Christians of the first century, that could speak of their martyrdom by being burned at the stake. It could refer to the fact that the Christians of that time and place were being blamed by Nero for burning Rome. It could describe the fact that these followers of Jesus were dragged from their families, dipped in tar, and used as living torches to light Nero's gardens. At the very least, it meant for them — and means for us — experiences of pain that compare to fire. Peter is talking about the things that assault you like a brushfire. They're usually out of control, and you know what they are in your life.

Peter mentioned one by name and summarized its sting with the word *reviled.* Some of you know what it's like to have your life shattered by that kind of pebble. You just label it differently. You see, to revile someone is to "insult them, to slander them, to dismantle their character with information that is not true." And we've felt those flames licking at our heels. And we've watched our world melt down because of the heat.

John Calvin understood this problem when he penned these words, "For sensitive people there is often more bitterness (and pain in such attacks) than in the loss of (physical) goods or in the torments or agonies of the body."[2]

He was right. Just maybe we can understand why Peter's sidekick, James, wrote that "the tongue is a *fire,* the very world of iniquity." By the way, how many fires did *you* start this week? I ask that because you may have felt the heat, and endured some damage lately. And no amount of special creams or bandages can take away the pain.

Peter suggests that the attack may have been a real shock, a surprise. But understand something here. Peter is not talking about the very normal and short-term surprise we all experience when the windows of our lives are shattered. He's not talking about those momentary shock waves that engulf us and cause us to wonder. The word *surprised* in the original language talks about a *continuing* never-get-over-it attitude of bewilderment and astonishment at what is happening.

Most of us evaluate some ordeals of life as strange, as out of place, as "I can't believe this is happening to me," but we get past it. Some of us get stuck in the mud and our wheels start spinning and our gears start stripping. Peter says, "Don't let that happen." Why not? Because hidden in the word *surprised* is not only the idea of feeling bewildered but also of then becoming resentful and bitter. Long-term bewilderment always marches us into long-term bitterness. And that is what worried Peter.

Should he be worried about you? The window of your life has been cracked. Something painful, something fiery has burst into your life and hurt you deeply. That happens to the best of us. But with you, it's different. You wouldn't let it go. Now, it won't let you go. And you're choking on your bitterness toward somebody, maybe toward God.

Peter says to you, "Don't be surprised. Your sufferings are not accidental — the heavenly computer board has not short-circuited. Your pain is not interfering with God's purposes for your life. In fact, it is part of His purpose."

I know that because the words *fiery ordeal and testing* in verse 12 have hiding in their background the meaning of a refining fire, a testing that produces a positive result. Peter is suggesting that the fires of suffering, if we'll allow them, will actually purify and strengthen us. In other words, when the pebbles of pain break into our lives, growth and maturity can occur.

A number of years ago, Malcolm Muggeridge had this good word to offer to us about affliction:

> I can say with complete truthfulness that everything I have learned in my seventy-five years in this world, everything that has truly enhanced and enlightened my existence, has been through affliction and not through happiness, whether pursued or attained. In other words, if it ever were to be possible to eliminate affliction from our earthly existence, the result would not be to make life delectable, but to make it too (trite, ordinary) and trivial to be endurable.[3]

My friends, when God our Refiner turns up the heat, His desire is to reshape us, to mold us, to cause us to grow up spiritually. And all of us must daily face the process of maturing, but that maturing takes heat.

Ruth Harms Calkin, in her little book, *Lord, Don't You Love Me Anymore?* puts this in perspective for us. These are her well-chosen words:

O God
Despite my deep desire to please You
In the midst of confinement and pain
There are so many temptations
That hover like a thick cloud
Over all my honest efforts.
Is there ever an escape, dear God,
From the subtle temptations

That accompany perpetual pain?
How can I avoid the clamoring thoughts
The weakness, the helplessness
The pricking irritations?
Then, dear God, there are the weary mornings
After sleepless nights.
The disturbing fears that cling so tightly.
How can I resist the "if onlys"
When the pain pierces with such intensity?

Over and over the question Why? creeps stealthily
Into the dark corners of my thoughts.
"Why *this*, dear God, when I long to serve You?"
"Why *this*, when in an instant You could make me well?"
And yet, dear God, I know I must stop brooding.
I must stop badgering.
You need not explain Your eternal purpose
In terms I can understand.
Help me to respond without murmuring
About Your method of molding me
For I can know with unshakable assurance
That my destiny is perfection
In the eternal presence of the living God.[4]

REDEFINING PAIN

That's where we want to be. But before we get there, before we can respond in mature fashion to the fires and pebbles, we need to be very clear on something. The pain that Peter encircles in these verses does not include *every kind* of pain and suffering that might enter your life. The refining aspect that God has in mind does not embrace a certain kind of suffering — the suffering that bursts through the front door of your life because you invited it in. Look, look at the *disclaimer* Peter has for us in verse 15:

> By no means let any of you suffer as a murderer, or thief, or evildoer, or a troublesome meddler.

The first three offenses in this verse refer to breaking the laws of society and suffering the consequences of that action. When that happens, don't say that you are "suffering for Jesus' sake or for the sake of righteousness." You're not. You're suffering because you broke the law. Now most of us, like our first-century cousins, would see this first triad of actions and agree, "Right! No Christian should be involved in those activities. And if they are, then that's too bad. It's their own fault."

And Peter was wise enough to figure we'd think that way, so he added a fourth activity that was his main concern from the beginning. The first three just ease us into this one. . . . and he's got us before we can backpedal out of the territory. Look at the end of verse 15 again, "or a troublesome meddler."

The word *meddler* doesn't require a Near Eastern linguistics team to explain it. Peter is talking about Christian busybodies who stick their noses into situations they shouldn't, about people who love to be on the inside of everything — in your life, my life, the life of the church. But their involvement always agitates. By interfering in the lives of others, meddlers disrupt the peace and harmony of a church, a family, an office, a choir, a committee.

And sooner or later, somebody lowers the boom. That person gets called on the carpet. Invariably, the person leaves that encounter and tells others of their tribe, "He's just picking on me because I'm a Christian," or, "I'm suffering for the Lord."

Peter said, "Call it whatever you want, but you are not suffering on behalf of Jesus Christ. You're suffering because of your own obnoxious behavior." And you see, meddlers with that kind of mentality never learn. There is no refining, no improving, no change of behavior. They just keep sticking their noses in where they don't belong and convincing themselves that their behavior is appropriate because it's the cross they have to bear.

Does that describe you? Are you a troublesome meddler?

Do you poke around in this and that, ruffling feathers, raising the dust, creating a stir, dividing and polluting with every move, with every syllable?

If you are, stop it! Your meddling is kicking up stones that are cracking the windows of others' lives. And that should not be. Peter thought it was important enough to insert it, like bologna in a sandwich, right in the middle of his talk to us about our pain, our suffering. He wanted to say it exactly when he did, so it would stick, so it would make us squirm a bit.

RESPONDING AS A CHRISTIAN

Having accomplished that, he comes back to the rest of us who are enduring the refining heat of God and addresses our perspective and our response. The first part of that response is in verse 13.

> But to the degree that you share the sufferings of
> Christ, keep on rejoicing; so that also at the revelation
> of His glory, you may rejoice with exultation.

When we suffer, we share "the sufferings of Christ." How is that? Think of it this way. The friends who are closest to you are those with whom you have suffered and hurt. As you stumbled and crawled through your pain together, you grew as friends. The same thing happens spiritually. As you view your righteous suffering as suffering for Him and with Him, you love Him more deeply and trust Him more completely.

Earlier in his letter Peter said that we have been called by Christ to follow His example in suffering. In other words, when we suffer and share that experience with Christ, it is an indication of our identification with Him.

Few men of this century have understood this better than Dietrich Bonhoeffer. He was executed by the direct order of Heinrich Himmler in April 1945, only a few days before the end of World War II. Before that he had written:

Suffering, then, is the badge of true discipleship. The disciple is not above his master. Following Christ means suffering because we have to suffer. Discipleship means allegiance to the suffering Christ, and therefore it is not at all surprising that Christians should be called upon to suffer. In fact, it is a joy and a token of his grace.[5]

Peter knew that. He even screwed up his courage and talked about the ability to have joy in the middle of our pain, "that also at the revelation of His glory, you may rejoice with exultation." Our joy, now in the teeth of pain, will of course be turned into super joy at the return of Jesus Christ. We'd expect Peter to say that. But he is talking about joy in pain right now.

Let's understand what he's driving at. It is clear from the Bible that rejoicing in suffering is not simply a grin-and-bear-it attitude, or a tough-it-out-and-see-how-much-you-can-take mind-set. Joy during pain is not just-hang-in-there or keep-a-stiff-upper-lip rhetoric. That's not it at all.

To know joy in our suffering is not a trick of the mind. *Suffering has meaning if it puts us in deep fellowship with Jesus Christ.* Joy is something that defies our circumstances and occurs in spite of them. Joy is a posture, a position. It is what one man called "that deep-settled confidence that God is in control of every area of my life."

The fullness of joy comes when we have a deep sense of the presence of God in our lives. Joy occurs when our pain pushes us to depend upon our God, not ourselves. Tim Hansel, a gifted Christian writer, goes to the heart of the matter this way:

Pain is inevitable, but misery is optional. We cannot avoid pain, but we can avoid joy. God has given us such immense freedom that He will allow us to be as miserable as we want to be.

I know some people who spend their entire lives practicing being unhappy, diligently pursuing joylessness. They get more mileage from having people feel sorry for them than from choosing to live out their lives in the context of joy.

Joy is simple (not to be confused with easy). At any moment in life we have at least two options, and one of them is to choose an attitude of gratitude, a posture of grace, a commitment to joy.[6]

It has been well said:

It was Augustine who said,
"A Christian should be an Alleluia
From head to foot."
Too often, Lord, I am a funeral dirge
Spreading gloom and pessimism,
Mixed with worry and fear.
Put a new song in my heart, God.
Give me a singing trust.
Remold and remake me
Into Your personal alleluia.[7]

There's something else about our response to suffering that we should keep in mind. Our attitude of joy does not come only from within ourselves. It's not something we just conjure up. There is a divine presence in us, whether we realize it or not, who assists us. Verse 14 helps us see that:

If you are reviled for the name of Christ, you are blessed, because the Spirit of glory and of God rests upon you.

The title, "the Spirit of glory and of God," is a reference to the indwelling presence of the Holy Spirit within all those who are believers in Jesus Christ. And when Peter says that the Holy Spirit "rests upon you," he means that the Spirit is within you continually. There isn't a moment in your life as a believer when you cannot draw upon the Spirit of God. Especially in moments of crisis, in times of deepest anguish, Peter insists that God's Spirit is available to strengthen you. And strength is exactly what you need when the pain is screaming at you.

But you've discovered, as I have, that all your stubbornness, all your willpower, all your determination, all your fighting spirit rolled together still leave you short, still leave you bailing water, especially when you are alone, late at night, when everybody else is counting sheep or dreaming dreams. *That's when you need to draw upon a strength that is not your own.* That's what Peter is talking about.

Her name was Lina Sandell. Swedish. Born in 1832. She loved her dad. Idolized him in fact. As she grew older she often ministered alongside of him. When she was only twenty-six, her father died. But he didn't just die. They were traveling together by ship, and were out on the deck surveying the beauty of creation. For some reason the ship lurched unsteadily and Lina Sandell's father fell overboard. Rescue was impossible. He drowned before her very eyes. And the one she loved, cherished, even idolized, was gone. That's when Lina Sandell dug deep within for help. She found it and wrote these familiar words:

> Day by day and with each passing moment,
> strength I find to meet my trials here.
> Trusting in my Father's wise bestowment,
> I've no cause for worry or for fear.
>
> He whose heart is kind beyond all measure,
> gives unto each day what He deems best.
> Lovingly it's part of pain and pleasure,
> mingling toil with peace and rest.[8]

REJOICING IN CHRIST

There's one more thing that embraces everything we've seen already, but it is worth noting again. You'll find it in verses 16-19. Just glance at verse 16 for now:

> If anyone suffers as a Christian, let him not feel ashamed, but in that name let him glorify God.

The name *Christian* appears only three times in the New

Testament, but it always identifies the followers of Jesus. Here Peter connects that name with suffering. In other words, these people are suffering because of their link with Jesus Christ. Either their lifestyle or their words invited abuse, persecution. Their sufferings blitzed their lives because they were being faithful to Christ.

When you stand at attention for integrity, for honesty, for moral values and positive ethics, you will feel the pain. When you do not stoop to slander, malice, revenge, or deceit, people will laugh. They may even attack. So, I wonder . . . what pain is now part of your life because you have stood at attention for Christ?

As that suffering accosts you, remember that it is the refining and purifying judgment of God in your life. It has redemptive value for you. Unbelieving persons, on the other hand, aren't feeling that refining judgment. The judgment they face is punishment. And when Christ returns they will face the fire of His anger in judgment. But that is not true for you who follow Him, who identify with His name. His link to you is one of love. It is a union that begs for you to trust Him.

> Therefore, let those also who suffer according to the will of God entrust their souls to a faithful Creator in doing what is right (v. 19).

The combination of *faithful* and *Creator* remind us of God's love and His power . . . in the midst of our pain. Christians do not suffer accidentally or because of irresistible forces of fate. We suffer according to God's will.

God created the world, and He has faithfully ordered it and sustained it since the creation. And because we know He is faithful, we can count on Him to fulfill His promises. If He can oversee the forces of nature, surely He can see us through the trials we face.

> Upon reflection, no better comfort in suffering can be found than this: it is God's good and perfect will. For therein lies the knowledge that there is a limit to the

suffering, both in its intensity and in its duration, a limit set and maintained by the God who is our Creator, our Savior, our Sustainer, our Father. And therein also lies the knowledge that this suffering is only for our good: it is purifying us, drawing us closer to our Lord, and making us more like Him in our lives. In all of it we are not alone, but we can depend on the care of a faithful Creator, we can rejoice in the fellowship of a Savior who also suffered; we can (delight) in the constant presence of a Spirit of glory who delights to rest upon us.[9]

When the pebbles bounce off the freeway of your life and crack the crystal-clear window of your circumstances, keep watching and looking. Your view will one day be clearer! In fact, that's what this book is all about. Reading it won't replace the cracked windows of your life, but I hope it helps you finish your journey.

Answer me when I call, O God of my righteousness!
Thou hast relieved me in my distress;
Be gracious to me and hear my prayer.

O sons of men, how long will my honor become a reproach?
How long will you love what is worthless
and aim at deception?
But know that the Lord has set apart
the godly man for Himself;
The Lord hears when I call to Him.

Tremble, and do not sin;
Meditate in your heart upon your bed, and be still.
Offer the sacrifices of righteousness,
And trust in the Lord.

Many are saying, "Who will show us any good?"
Lift up the light of thy countenance upon us, O Lord!
Thou hast put gladness in my heart,
More than when their grain and new wine abound.
In peace I will both lie down and sleep,
For Thou alone, O Lord, dost make me to dwell in safety.
Psalm 4

2

When You Can't Hide the Pain

In Aspen Colorado, on March 18, 1979, a twin-engined plane crashed shortly after takeoff. At that moment, Mrs. Stephanie Ambrose May lost her husband, John Edward, fifty-one years old and chief executive officer and chairman of the board of May Petroleum. A business and civic leader in Dallas, he had a doctorate from SMU and had completed Harvard's advanced management program. In the plane with him were their son, David Edward, age twenty-two, a senior at the University of Texas, majoring in petroleum engineering; their daughter, Karla Emily, age eighteen; and a son-in-law, Richard Owen Snyder.

For the next two months Mrs. May kept a diary in which she recorded her feelings, her emotions. She wrote this two months after the accident:

My burden is heavy, but I don't walk alone. My pain is unrelenting, but I thank God for every moment that He blessed me with. I pray that my life will be used for His glory, that I might carry my burden with Christian dignity, and that *out of my devastation* may His kingdom become apparent to someone lost and in pain. I close this diary, and with it goes all my known ability and capacity for love. I cannot replace or compare my loss. It is my loss. I am not strong. I am not

33

brave. I am a Christian with a burden to carry and a
message to share. I have been severely tested, but my
faith has survived, and I have been strengthened in
my love and devotion to the Lord. O God, my life is
Yours—comfort me in Your arms and direct my life. I
have *walked in hell*, but now I walk with God in
peace. John Edward, David, Karla, and Richard are in
God's hands. I am in God's arms. His love surrounds
me. *This rose will bloom again.*[1]

Mrs. Stephanie Ambrose May's diary reads very much
like another journal you are familiar with. Though separated in time by nearly 3,000 years, both echo off the walls of
hearts in pain. Though written in circumstances so removed
from each other that it at first seems almost impossible to
connect them, still they are joined by anguish, an invisible
thread that transcends time and place and touches our
hearts.

That other diary is the Old Testament book we call the
Psalms. Many of the psalms include, on the one hand, the
writers' own inner emotions of *discouragement, anxiety, du-
ress and fear.* As I read them, I wonder how they understand my world, my pain so well. But on the other hand,
the psalms also record a thankful joy even in the face of
opposition, even in the darkened fog that swallows us up
when God allows the vice of pain to tighten in our lives.
Like Mrs. May's diary, the psalms sound, even in their
most desperate moments, as if the writers were in the very
presence of God. In fact, it is interesting to note that the
Hebrew title for the Book of Psalms is "The Songs of
Praise."

You may be interested to know that not all the psalms
were written by Israel's King David. Many were, including
our text, but other people contributed out of their joy and
pain to the ancient hymnal—from Moses to a man named
Asaph, and even Solomon. Written over the course of 900
years, the psalms touch people in all places and in all types
of extremities.

A CALL FOR HELP

Martin Luther once wrote, "We should never lay aside the Book of Psalms, but should constantly view ourselves in it, as in a mirror, for we cannot appreciate its great glory unless we read it with diligence."[2]

And that is exactly what I'd like us to do as we attempt to relive the experience of David in Psalm 4. Look at verse 1, where David calls for help:

Answer me when I call, O God of my righteousness!
Thou hast relieved me in my distress; Be gracious to
me and hear my prayer.

The verb *to call* means simply "to cry out for help." David turned to prayer with trouble clouding his mind. All he knew to do was to go to God. All he wanted at this moment was that God would hear him and give him some peace of mind . . . some answers. This important psalm addresses a basic human experience — the pain of suffering unjustly and being oppressed. Those are rough spots to be in, because they can turn a person away from God. And that is why there is something here we should not miss. In David's plea for an answer, there lies a hidden anguish — that God would not answer him. As one commentator suggests, "It seemed (to David) as if God was not lending an ear and was not going to answer (him). His prayers seemed to ricochet off the ceiling of his life."[3]

I don't think there are many people who haven't experienced this — especially when the pain and the panic are protracted. I know I've felt as if nothing I prayed got past the ozone layer.

And what made it worse for David is that he believed in his heart that God knew he was innocent, that the pain he was enduring at the time was not his fault. That's why in verse 1 he addressed the Lord as "the God of my righteousness" — the God who knew David was in the right. The anguish he felt was not the result of something he had done. Rather, it was the direct result of the words and actions of people he loved.

And so he cried out in desperation, "Answer me, Lord . . . please, be gracious to me and listen!" We've shouted that and worse in times of distress, haven't we? And we have felt locked out of heaven. The moments of desperation that have rocked me the most were the ones when I knew, in my heart of hearts, that I was innocent before God. I zigged when I should have zagged. As a matter of fact, I had flown straight as an arrow. Still, the pain continued to march after me.

That is where David stood as he lifted his voice to heaven and cried for help. What made him question God's interest in his life? There were three related circumstances that prompted his desperate cry.

● The first one, at the end of verse 1, is not so much a statement of fact as it is still a cry for help. The text of the Hebrew is best understood as, "When I am in distress . . . give me some relief." The word *distress* means "to be in a tight spot, to be pressed." In some places it is translated, "I am in anguish."

As David put his thoughts to paper at the end of his day, he was fighting with a rebellious son. Absalom, through treachery and back-stabbings, had wrenched the throne of Israel away from his own father, and now David, with a handful of loyal followers, was on the run in the wilderness. All day long David fled with his men, looking all the time over his shoulder for a distant cloud of dust which would indicate pursuit. Chuck Swindoll speaks to such pain:

> Of all life's pressures, none is harder to bear than trouble at home. Financial pressure is tough but not impossible to work out. Physical pain is bad—sometimes horrible—but usually not without hope. The loss of a job or failure at school may bring to the surface those feelings of desperation, yet they, too, will pass. But there is really nothing to compare with the lingering, agonizing, torturous heartache brought on by a

rebellious and wayward child. Too big to spank. Too angry to reason with. Too volatile to threaten. Too stubborn to warn. Bound and determined to run free of authority . . . regardless. . . .

If you have been there, no one needs to (elaborate). The brokenhearted mom and dad need a comforter, not a commentator. It is agony at its highest peak. . . . Prayer becomes a lonely vigil. . . . at times, an empty, hopeless, repetition of sounds struggling out of a swollen face. Thoughts are confused and endless.

"Where did we go wrong? Will we ever see each other again? Is he/she safe? If we had it to do over again. How did it all start? Should we . . . could we?"[4]

When my own brother put his life on hold for eight years through drugs and alcohol, I sensed some of David's desperation. Today my brother loves the Lord and is following after Him, but that's now. It wasn't always like that. Then there were the police, the questions, the accusations. There were times of anger, hours of panic, days of fear . . . wondering, "Is he alive?"

One can go for just so long in the face of outright opposition from people and circumstances before there is a slow crumbling of resolve or resistance. And that is doubly true when the opposition comes from your own family, as it did with David. Feeling hemmed in and attacked, he asked God to give him room, to release him from the pressure, the distress.

● Not only was there distress in his life, but tagging along, like a dog barking at his heels, were *dishonor* and *deception.* Let's consider them together, remembering that they are related to what we've seen. Look at verse 2:

O sons of men, how long will my honor become a reproach? How long will you love what is worthless and aim at deception? Selah.

Honor refers to a person's good name and positive reputation. David's reputation was being undermined. It was being dishonored. When he said that his "honor became a

reproach," he meant that his reputation was in shambles; it
was worthless. He may have been referring to his reputation as king or as a military leader. It doesn't look very good
when a king is on the run. But maybe, just maybe, he was
also talking about his reputation as a father. Here was his
own son using slander and deception to turn people against
him.

How do you feel when a family member betrays you?
When they rebel against you? When they run counter to
everything you believe in? And when they actively seek to
destroy your reputation, to boot? How do you feel?

Someone has said, "When wealth is lost, nothing is lost.
When health is lost, something is lost; when character is
lost, all is lost."[5] David felt that way. In verse 2 he responded by shouting, "How long will this continue?" The emphasis of the Hebrew is, "Why are you doing this to me?" You
see, not only was Absalom turning on David, but others
joined in. They are described at the end of verse 2, "How
long will you love what is worthless and aim at deception?"

These men loved "sham" and as a result, freely propagat-
ed hollow and empty charges against an innocent man. And
they didn't just slide into that kind of treatment; the text
says they aimed at deception. The verb for *aim at* suggests
they worked hard to come up with lies. They lay awake at
night plotting how to inflict pain. They went out of their
way to see David squirm.

One commentator describes the scene vividly, "David
knew the sudden stab of pain that keeps you awake at
night. Yesterday with its taunts, the spectacle of disloyalty,
cold fear, the sense of loneliness and isolation . . . the
awareness of the strength behind the rebellion horrified
him."[6]

You'll notice in the title of this psalm that it is an evening
prayer. That tells us that David wrote this after a long and
anguished day. He looked back over what had transpired . . .
and he couldn't believe it. Just like some of you. There are
days for all of us which need a psalm like this, especially

when we have been betrayed. Something lying close to our souls cannot indulge treason, not even trivial treason. We feel fouled and diminished. A human relationship built on trust is fractured by betrayal. We know it is so because we feel the stab so deeply. Very much like the woman who wrote this letter:

> For twenty-two years I've built the business. I married a man and brought him in. I became vice-president and made him president. A few years later, when we got involved in divorce litigation, he brought in a sharp lawyer. He transferred all our assets and liabilities into a new corporation. Suddenly I was out of the corporation which I had founded and built. I had nothing to show for more than thirty years of labor. Anger, resentment, jealousy, you name it . . . I've had to deal with all of it because I have crashed. But I can't live that way; that way I'll perish.

SOME WAYS TO COPE

We've all experienced those emotions in the face of distress, dishonor, and deception. But like that woman we can't live that way or it will destroy us. David would have agreed. Something had to give; something had to change. It did. But there is no suggestion in this psalm that the accusers went away or that they stopped their lies and deception. What changed, as a result of his prayer, was *not the external* circumstances, but the inner heart of David, and that change led him to some practical conclusions that should help us cope.

● The first conclusion, we could summarize under the word *reflect.* In situations of distress, dishonor, and deception, we must always reflect on the fact that God loves us. David does that in verse 3:

> But know that the Lord has set apart the godly man for Himself; the Lord hears when I call to Him.

The words *set apart* mean that God had "marvelously chosen" David. He was reminding himself and his enemies that the one they were attacking was loved by God. Even as David wrote, he was beginning to answer his own doubts. In verse 1 he wondered whether God cared about him. But now as he reflected upon the love of God, he realized that it applied to himself. And so what began as a cry of doubt, a cry of help, ended up as a statement of confidence. Through reflection, David was beginning to understand that.

But that doesn't immediately take away the pain, the sting, or the anger, does it? David knew this and that's why he continued. The *New International Version* of the Bible gives an excellent rendering of the first part of verse 4, "In your anger, do not sin." The Septuagint, the first translation of the Hebrew Bible into Greek some 200 years before Christ, says, "Be angry, but do not sin." And the true sense of the verb is "to tremble or stand in awe," "to be disturbed, agitated, angry." Distress, dishonor, and deception hurt. Often with that hurt there is anger.

Dr. Willard Gaylin says, "When those we depend on for love and support truly betray that trust, we are outraged . . . "[7] We all know how our hearts can grow bitter at night over some injustice we have experienced. So David says, "You can tremble with anger and rage, but don't sin with your actions!" Admit that you're angry . . . don't deny it, but don't let it control you. Instead of allowing that anger to consume us, notice verse 4:

Meditate in your heart upon your bed and be still.

When you are hurt and angry, you need a time to be quiet, a time to process those feelings. The verb *meditate* means "to think, to reflect back." It suggests that you find some time in the midst of the pain to think carefully about who you are . . . and who God is. The sense of the verse is, "Let the still hours of the night bring calmer and wiser thoughts with them."

Thank You for this quiet time
when the moments drop away into forever,
plopping like spatters of rain upon a window pane.
Thank You that here within the stillness I can
think . . .
I can try to understand the changes inside me —
in my feelings, in my thoughts, in my beliefs.
Thank You, Lord that You have found me here
and have filled the empty space of my heart.[8]

Are you ever so mad you can taste it? You hurt so bad you're ready to explode? That's a good time to get alone and talk to God. To tell Him exactly how you feel and why. It is not wrong to come to Him that way. It is better, much better, to bring it to God than to turn it into a barrier that shuts God out. There is no better time to approach God than when you are bewildered and hurting. Should you fail to come to Him, you may become twisted, bitter, useless. But if you bring Him your hurts and confusion, a number of things will happen. Your mind and spirit will begin to clear. You will begin to think properly again. And your faith will deepen as you reflect on who it is who loves you.

● When that happens, David's second conclusion may not seem quite so difficult:

Offer the sacrifices of righteousness, and trust in the Lord (v. 5).

You've seen it happen. When you feel wronged, you also feel you have a right to demand justice. And sometimes you believe that justice can be accomplished only when you can hurt those who have hurt you, disappoint those who have disillusioned you, make suffer those who have injured and given you pain. You may have gone to great efforts to avenge a wrongdoing, only to find out that once you have your revenge, you have accomplished little more than finding yourself loveless and alone. David would have you go another way . . . the way of trust. He talks about offering "sacrifices of righteousness." That means giving up your

claims and no longer seeking your own way. In essence, it
is the same as trusting God with your future. The word that
David chose for *trust* is interesting. It comes from a verb
that means "to throw yourself down on your face, to lie
extended on the ground." The picture is that of throwing
yourself on God.

It is so hard to trust when you want to strike back, when
you want to fight for your reputation, your honor. It is
difficult to ease up when you have been hurt, when you're
under pressure. But there comes a time when you need to
trust God to take care of things His way. Centuries ago,
Thomas à Kempis said it well:

> There is no great reliance to be placed in a frail and
> mortal man, though he may be helpful and dear to us;
> neither should we be much grieved, if at times he
> should be against us and contradict us. Those who are
> with you today may be against you tomorrow and the
> opposite may be the case, for men often change like
> the wind. Place your whole trust in the Lord; let Him
> alone be your fear and your love. He Himself will
> answer for you and will do what is best for you.[9]

Will you do that? Will you stop your fighting? Stop pressing . . . pushing . . . dividing? What good is it accomplishing?

Now you may be thinking, "That sounds good, but I still
wonder if things will ever work out!" David had some
friends who thought along those lines. While he was on the
run with them, they came to him with their nagging doubts.
Look at the first part of verse 6:

Many are saying,"Who will show us any good?"

When things didn't turn around quickly in David's circumstances, people started coming at David . . . and they
kept on coming and they kept on saying, "This isn't going
to work out." They had degenerated into defeat and pessimism and were adding to David's problems.

G. Campbell Morgan, commenting on this verse, writes,
"This is the language of a person, who, looking back, is

dissatisfied, looking around is full of cynicism, and looking on is pessimistic. It is the language of restlessness and dissatisfaction."[10]

When the guns are being fired at you, the pressure tends to sort out your friends. I've noticed in my life how quickly some who I was sure were on my team, when the heat was on, ended up on the other side or, at best, were skeptical of me as an individual of honor. They sometimes talked like David's "friends."

Yet, we all lean that way, do we not? Overnight, it seems, we are no longer young . . . and we look back. All our life we used to look forward in hope, but now we start looking back, no longer speaking in terms of hope, but in terms of "ifs:"

–If I had taken a different road . . .
–If I had married a different person . . .
–If I had done business differently . . .

• David's friends felt that pull and told him about it. So what did he conclude? He concluded that along with his trust in God there must also be his own *attitude of joy.* Look at the rest of verse 6 and then verse 7:

Lift up the light of Thy countenance upon us, O Lord!
Thou hast put gladness in my heart,
More than when their grain and new wine abound.

The expression, "Lift up the light of Thy countenance," is a Hebrew way of asking that God's presence once again become real to him. David knew what we sometimes forget—that a conscious awareness of God's presence in our lives will produce joy. You see, joy is the experience of gratitude, of being glad for life in the presence of the Giver of Life.

J.I. Packer, in his wonderful book, *Hot Tub Religion,* helps me understand this when he offers this counsel,

Joy: A delight in life that runs deeper than pain or pleasure . . . not limited by nor tied solely to external circumstances . . . a gift of God . . . a quality of life and not simply a fleeting emotion. *The fullness of joy comes when there is a deep sense of the presence of God in one's life.*[11]

That is what David concluded . . . that is what he prayed for . . . an awareness of God's presence in his life to produce an inner joy that would be greater than the external, syrupy joy that society offers. Did you catch that in verse 7? "Thou hast put gladness in my heart, More than when their grain and new wine abound." David contrasted this new joy with the joy his enemies had when they experienced the highest joy they were capable of—joy linked to material possessions—in their case, food and drink.

As long as things rolled along without a hitch in their lives, they had what they called joy. But that's not what it was. David had joy in spite of his circumstances. You see, even as he wrote this verse, he was on the run. He and his men were in desperate need of food, because Absalom and his crew had seized all the supplies. Still, David "was surprised by joy," as C.S. Lewis would say. Are we? Joy is the gigantic secret of the believer that should mark our lives. I am always astounded at the emphasis in the Word on joy. Peter spotted it, as we saw in chapter 1, and now David. James will hitchhike joy to pain in the next chapter. And others have followed in their train. Several years ago Lloyd Ogilvie wrote these amazing words:

> This past year has been the most difficult year of my life. My wife has been through five major surgeries, radiation treatment, and chemotherapy. I am thankful that I now know she is going to make it. During the same year, I suffered the loss of several key staff teammates whose moves were very guided for them, but a source of pressure and uncertainty in my work. Problems which I could have tackled with gusto under normal circumstances seemed to loom in all directions. Discouragement lurked around every corner, trying to capture my feelings. Prayer was no longer a contem-

plative luxury, but the only way to survive. My own intercessions were multiplied by the prayers of others. Friendships were deepened as I was forced to allow people to assure me with words I had preached for years. No day went by without a conversation, letter, or phone call giving me love and hope. The greatest discovery is that I can have joy when I don't feel like it — artesian joy.[12]

● That brings us to David's final conclusion. It is the inevitable one. After *reflecting* on God's care for him, after throwing himself upon his God in *trust,* and after discovering a heart of joy even in the midst of intense pain, he was then able to *relax.*

In peace I will both lie down and sleep, For Thou alone, O Lord, dost make me to dwell in safety (v. 8).

Where the lies and slanders of his son and others had created an inner tension and pressures that made sleep impossible, the Lord now provided David with an *inner security and joy* that allowed him to sleep. David was saying, "I'm sleeping again, not harassed by disturbing and anxious thoughts." Although he was still betrayed and rejected by so many who were close to him, so much so that he was forced to live almost completely alone, yet now David felt perfectly safe. "David concludes by stating that as he is protected by the power of God, he enjoys as much security and peace as if he had been defended by all the (armies) on the earth."[13]

THE GREATEST RESOURCE

My friends, when we are distressed . . . and we all are, when we are deceived . . . and we all have been, we can still be delighted if we remember that we have a relationship that can never be changed: we are children of the Most High. We have a resource that can never be dimin-

ished: the power of the Spirit of God. We have a peace that
can never be destroyed: it is the God of Peace Himself. We
have a joy that can never be surpassed: the Bible calls it
"joy unspeakable and full of glory." We have a love that
will never let us go: God's unconditional love. We have a
sovereign Lord who can never lose control: the King of
kings Himself.

A friend of our family who understands pain and rejection recently wrote this letter:

I must tell you about a very special three-year-old in
my Sunday School class named Timmy. God is working through this little guy to keep me seeing what is
right in my life, not just the negatives. Several weeks
ago we had the story of Jesus healing the palsied man
let down through the roof by his friends. As I prepared
for this and read the Scripture, I was impressed with
how easy it was for our Lord to heal this man. I said,
"Lord, it was so easy for You there. Could You just slip
a little miracle in for me too and heal me?"

Well, the next morning in Sunday School we just
got to the part where the man is healed, picks up his
bed and goes home when dear Timmy jumped off his
chair and excitedly interrupted me with, "Teecho,
Jesus can make yo legs work too, huh?" And the big-
gest smile was just from ear to ear on his face, he was
so excited!! His statement made me stop for a bit and I
had to restate what I knew in my heart, "Yes, Jesus
can make Miss Laura walk too, but it has to be when
Jesus wants it to happen."

The next week was the story of ten lepers Jesus
healed and only one said, "Thank You." Well, just as
we got to that exciting part of the healing, precious
Timmy was waving his arms at me, "Miss Laura, do yo
legs work yet?" I replied, "No, not yet, but we'll keep
asking Jesus and He'll make them work when He says
so." Timmy had to hear something more. "Well, are
they just a leetle bit betto?" "Yes, sweetheart, my legs
are a little better."

On Easter Sunday I was praying my way through the hour because of added pain, struggles, etc. I was sitting in a chair ready to start another activity (and not counting *all* of my blessings) when Timmy came over, grabbed both of my arms and said, "Hey! Miss Laura, you awms aw all betto!" He was so excited as he looked intently at my arms. "Timmy, my arms were always okay, remember? It's my legs that don't work," I replied. "Noooo," he said, "Don't you remembo? You had those things on them." Then I remembered the tendonitis and splints, etc. that I'd worn for several weeks. I was so preoccupied with the current problem that I failed to see the past answers to prayer. Then I hugged this little guy and told him of how Jesus made my arms "betto" and that we needed to tell Jesus "Thank You!"

How weary our Lord must become when we, like the nine lepers, fail to say, "Thank you!" for answers to prayer. By the way, this little guy is from a broken home where both sides have remarried. Timmy prays in my class, "Dear Jesus, please make my mommy and daddy not *awgue* so much. Amen." This is my mission field, teaching these little precious hearts about our dear Savior. It is an honor and privilege!

*James, a bond-servant of God and of the Lord Jesus Christ, to
the twelve tribes who are dispersed abroad, greetings.*

*Consider it all joy, my brethren, when you encounter
various trials, knowing that the testing of your
faith produces endurance. And let endurance
have its perfect result, that you may be
perfect and complete, lacking in nothing.*

*But if any of you lacks wisdom, let him ask of God,
who gives to all men generously, and without
reproach, and it will be given to him.*

James 1:1-5

3

When the Bottom Falls Out

Their circumstances are as different as their responses. Some of the responses are more understandable than others, but they include us all.

Gladys Burr was only thirty years old. She had an impediment of speech and she was in a state hospital. Suddenly they transferred her to a state training center for mentally disturbed patients. The psychiatrist examined her and found her competent, and yet she was retained as a patient for four years. From then on, she was farmed out as a mentally retarded person, from one home to another. At age seventy-two she was released; the finding was that she had only an impediment of speech. She was never mentally disabled. She is suing her state for $125 million.

Wang Yuenken escaped with his wife and four children from Vietnam as boat people. At sea they were shipwrecked on a very small island. He and his wife saw their four children starve to death. Cannibalism was practiced among some of the survivors. When asked if he wants to comment on their circumstances, Wang says, "There are no tears left; that is passed. There is nothing I can do about it."[1]

Philip often had his glass of apple juice and a muffin, along with his sister and the other children while his mother and other women had tea or coffee before their Thursday morning Bible class. Bright blue eyes full of response and sparkle, a shock of thick blond hair and pink cheeks spoke of a robust, healthy three-year-old with a zest for life. His five-year-old sister, Gwen, was playing by his bed during his seemingly minor illness, croup, when he choked and within seconds his breathing stopped. "Mother, Mother, Philip has gone." Gwen instinctively understood that her brother was no longer in the room with her. His body was there, but Philip was out of her reach. But how could that be?[2]

A letter from Nebraska comments on a picture: (The picture) makes me think of my brother's family. A tornado swept the buildings and all away. They were in nightclothes, barefoot, just after midnight. They were scattered, and walking around through splinters, barbed wire. By calling, they finally all found each other. Their car had been blown away, but getting out on the road, they were able to stop a car to take them to the hospital twenty miles away. Their seven-month-old baby had a wood splinter through his chest, and died before morning. This little boy has on his gravestone these words:

Precious jewel, bright gem for His crown.

So may the Lord's name be glorified.

As I look back through the file of pain that opened when my fifteen-year-old brother-in-law died, I'm not sure that I could have written such an epitaph, though I would have wanted to be able to. But when the bottom falls out of our lives, we react in different ways. It might be safe to say that we have concluded that there are as many different and appropriate responses to the difficulties of life as there are difficulties. But in so concluding, we may have lost an understanding of the best response.

SCATTERED AND BATTERED PEOPLE

I think James, the half brother of Jesus Christ, understood our natural tendencies. As a pastor and leader of the church in the city of Jerusalem, he had an ability to read people and to walk with them when life was difficult. He was not so removed that he could not understand. In fact, he understood so well that he wrote about it in the New Testament letter that bears his name, the Epistle of James. It is a very practical book, written to deal with the hardships of life. James is one of the Bible's greatest realists. And it is highly significant that this down-to-earth James would begin his letter by encouraging his readers to respond differently than others, when the bottom fell out of life.

We need to listen to James because the pressures in our age are great. Many people cannot cope with the difficulties they must face and often seek to escape from the problems that confront them. But in many instances they find that escape is impossible and that, in fact, they cannot control their lives.

In addressing a *scattered* and *battered* group of Christians in century one, James really reached out across the distance of time to our century, and to our situation, to sit with us in the family rooms of our lives. He understands well our feeling of being scattered. Look at verse 1 of his epistle:

> James, a bond-servant of God and of the Lord Jesus Christ, to the twelve tribes who are dispersed abroad, greetings.

James was writing to Jewish people who had accepted Jesus Christ as their Savior. Originally, they lived in Jerusalem, where James pastored, but now they were scattered to other cities and countries. As religious persecution intensified in Jerusalem, they had been forced to leave, simply to survive. And as a result, families and long-time friends were inevitably separated, as everyone left to start over again.

If you have ever been forced to move from a place you identify as home, from a city where you were involved, and perhaps from a church where you ministered to and were cared for, you understand scattering. Perhaps you were forced to move because of unemployment, or a job transfer, or a company merger or buy-out. Perhaps the reasons were health-related. Or maybe you moved "on a hope and prayer" that life would be better in the new place, and you understand how being scattered easily translates into loneliness and feelings of isolation. You seem lost, cut off. You feel as if nobody in this new place truly notices you or cares about you. And you want to go back, but you can't. You feel ignored and therefore insignificant, even though you are surrounded by people.

I understand the trauma of being scattered. I remember the day our family moved from Arizona to Ohio. Patricia was to fly on to Denver a day later where she was to be involved in a conference for wives of senior pastors, and so it was my task to head out with our two boys and the dog. Some friends gathered at the house to wish us well. Then fifteen minutes before we took off, one of my friends said, "I'll take some time off work and drive to Albuquerque with you. Let's go!" And we did. That first day's drive was great, but the next morning my friend had to leave. I wept . . . for two days. I did not want to move, to leave. I understand scattering. Do you? Perhaps Frederick W. Robertson described you when he wrote:

> There are times when hands touch ours, but only send an icy chill of unsympathizing indifference to the heart: when eyes gaze into ours, but with a glazed look which cannot read into the bottom of our souls — when words pass from our lips, but only come back as an echo (as if) replying through a dreary solitude when the multitudes throng and press us, and (yet) we cannot say, as Christ said, "Someone touched me." For the only contact has been not between soul and soul, but only between form and form.[3]

Thomas Wolfe once put it this way, "Loneliness, far from being a rare and curious phenomenon peculiar to myself and a few other solitary men, is the central and inevitable fact of human existence."[4] But what makes our scattering worse . . . is that we also sometimes have to face being *battered* at the same time.

> Consider it all joy, my brethren when you encounter various trials (v. 2).

James is not dealing with theoretical issues here. He doesn't say "if" you encounter trials, but "when" you encounter them. That means that they are inevitable and unavoidable. They often surround us and offer no conceivable escape. And more than that, this verse indicates that their arrival cannot be pinpointed ahead of time. The pain that comes from trials is likely to hit us without a moment's warning. One commentator suggested, "Any day, at any time of day, some experience of trial is, as it were, lying in wait ready to leap on us so that we shout, 'What is this?' or 'Why is this happening to me?' "[5]

Now it wouldn't be so bad if we could at least restrict their scope or choose the category of difficulty. But we can't. James knew this. That's why he talked about encountering *various* trials. The word means "diversified, complex and intricate" problems. In other words, all kinds of problems. For the people of James' day, that translated into illnesses, financial reversals, and social and economic hardships. Whatever problem they could imagine, that is what they might face. And it wouldn't be something they could anticipate — they would just stumble into it. The verb *encounter* in this verse describes "falling into the midst of people, objects or circumstances that are painful."

So it was for James' friends. . . . and for us. In the next thirty minutes 285 children will become victims of broken homes; parents will beat, molest, or otherwise abuse 228 children; 685 teenagers will take some form of narcotics; 57 kids will run away from their homes and 105 new people will try cocaine. Rose Bird, California's former Chief Justice, has said, "Ours is an amphetamine society, without the stability of an anchor, hurtling from one idea to another, momentarily clinging to them for support, but then discarding them."[6]

The same tone of desperation impacts Christians too. Eugene Peterson describes our dilemma in this way:

> No sooner have we plunged, expectantly and enthusiastically, into the river of Christian faith than we get our noses full of water and come up coughing and choking. No sooner do we confidently stride out on to the road of faith than we trip on an obstruction and fall to the hard surface, bruising our knees and elbows. For many, the first great surprise of the Christian life is in the form of troubles we meet. Somehow it is not what we supposed: we had expected something quite different; we had our minds set on Eden or on New Jerusalem. We are rudely awakened to something very different and we look around for help, scanning the horizon for someone who will give us aid.[7]

If we could honestly share our lives with each other, we would hear how varied our suffering is. Some of you are feeling the pain of a lingering illness or an untimely death of a loved one. Some of you know the constant ache of a marriage falling apart, or an unfulfilled romance, a rebellious child or an alcoholic parent. Some of you are struggling with overwhelming problems in your business or at school, a depression that will not go away, or a habit that you cannot seem to break. You feel as if the rug has been pulled out from under your feet, as if you're going to break apart at any moment.

RESPONDING WITH JOY

When we arrive at the point that everything inside of us screams, we often respond negatively. But there is a better response. It begins with our attitude . . . "Consider it all joy." James was very concerned that these believers progress to a mature, stable faith; to do so, they needed to maintain a distinctively Christian attitude toward problems. That attitude is inherent in the verb *consider* which means "to be precise, definite and decisive." When you consider, you reach a settled conviction in your mind about trials. To consider it all joy means you respond with a deliberate and intelligent appraisal.

As Christians we are to look at life from God's perspective and realize that a trial is not a wonderful experience in itself, but is the means of producing something valuable in us. James does not tell us to enjoy our trials, nor say that we must feel joyful. He is not asking us to break into mindless laughter when we are under the pile. Rather, he is saying that when the pressures come, we can face them with joy if we think carefully about the results they can produce in our life.

We need to remember that joy is something which defies circumstances and happens in spite of difficult circumstances. Whereas happiness is a feeling, joy is an attitude, a posture, a position. In the words of Elton Trueblood, "The Christian is joyful, not because he is blind . . . to suffering, but because he is convinced that [circumstances], in the light of divine sovereignty, are never ultimate. He is convinced that the unshakable purpose is the divine rule to things. . . . Though he can be sad, and is often perplexed, he is never really worried."[8]

J.B. Phillips, in his paraphrase of James, exposes the heartbeat of this verse, "When all kinds of trials . . . crowd into your lives, my brothers, don't resent them as intruders, but welcome them as friends!" The appropriate response to the varied trials that assault us is to view them as opportunities, under God's grace, for growth and development.

Most of the Old Testament psalms were born out of difficulty. Most of the New Testament epistles of Paul were written from prison. Most of the greatest thoughts of the greatest thinkers of history had to be refined through fire. Bunyan wrote *Pilgrim's Progress* from jail. Florence Nightingale, too sick to move from her bed, reorganized the

hospitals of England. Semiparalyzed and under the constant menace of apoplexy, Louis Pasteur was tireless in his
attack on disease. Sometimes it seems that when God is
about to greatly use someone, He puts them through the
fire. I love what the poet wrote ...

When God wants to drill a man,
And thrill a man,
And skill a man;
When God wants to mold a man
To play the noblest part,

When He yearns with all His heart
To create so great and bold a man
That all the world shall be amazed,
Watch His methods, watch His ways —
How He ruthlessly perfects
Whom He royally elects.

How He hammers him and hurts him,
And with mighty blows, converts him
Into trial shapes of clay,
Which only God understands,
While his tortured heart is crying,
And he lifts beseeching hands.

How He bends but never breaks
When his good He undertakes.
How He uses whom He chooses,
And with every purpose, fuses him,
By every act, induces him
To try His splendor out.
God knows what He's about.[9]

DEVELOPING ENDURANCE

The first element of our response is an attitude of joy. That
attitude is assisted by the second part of our response,

" ... knowing that the testing of your faith produces endurance" (v. 3).

Faith is central to the Christian life. Saving faith is living and active, and proves that it is alive by what it does and what it endures. Let me try to explain it this way.

We say that we believe that God is our Father, and that He is in control of our lives and cares for us. But as long as we remain untested, our belief falls short of day-to-day reality. But suppose the day comes — as it will — when circumstances seem to mock our belief, when the cruelty of life denies God's faithfulness, His silence calls into question His power, and the sheer haphazard, meaningless jumble of events in our lives challenges the possibility that God is even awake. What about our faith then? Sometimes it is precisely at that point that we struggle the most.

In his book *A Grief Observed*, C.S. Lewis honestly expresses how many of us respond at that moment:

> Meanwhile, where is God? Go to Him when your need is desperate, when all other help is vain, and what do you find? A door slammed in your face, and a sound of bolting and double bolting on the inside. After that, silence. You may as well turn away. The longer you wait, the more emphatic the silence will become.[10]

That's how it seems, unless we acknowledge that even through that test God is working on us to produce a deeper, stronger, more certain faith that is characterized by what James calls *endurance*. You see, it is in struggling against difficulties and opposition that spiritual stamina is developed. That is why James chose the word *endurance*, for it speaks of tenacity and stick-to-it-iveness. But endurance means far more than simply toughing it out. This is not merely a reference to passive resignation which is content to wait with bowed head until the troubles have run their course. It means "to steel oneself ... to hold fast to God and not to mistake His power and faithfulness, to abide under a load," grateful for the opportunity to endure, knowing that it will bring glory to God.

Significantly, this characteristic is only developed in the face of opposition. It cannot exist without testing. John Calvin was so right when he wrote, "It is better to limp *in* the way, than to run with swiftness *out* of it."

I couldn't help but think of a young man, Carl Joseph who comes from Madison, Florida, a town of 3,000. In 1980, when he finished high school, he received eight letters for athletics: three in football, three in track, and two in basketball. He plays nose guard in football, both offense and defense. In the 1979 season he was responsible for blocking two punts, two intended passes, and sacking the quarterback a number of times.

Carl Joseph was born without a leg. The right leg is there; the left leg is simply missing. He doesn't even have a thigh. When he is asked about his handicap, he says, "What handicap? I'm not handicapped." When he's asked about the spirit that caused the whole town to come together in May of 1980 to honor him, and Bear Bryant to leave Alabama and to come to shake his hand and to proclaim him "an exceptional young man," Carl Joseph attributes everything he is, everything he has accomplished, to the Lord Jesus Christ. He understands that the testing of our faith produces endurance.

MOVING TOWARD MATURITY

Now you might be saying, "I understand the need for a change of attitude, and I can even see the value of endurance in my life, but I want to see results now. I don't want to have to go through all this pain." If your mind is drifting in that direction   then you need to consider the third element of our response. It's found in verse 4:

> And let endurance have its perfect result, that you may be perfect and complete, lacking nothing.

The goal of testing is to produce maturity. That is what the words *perfect* and *complete* refer to. The point is that a Christian may be spiritually mature in many respects, but not complete if he/she has no endurance during adversity. In fact, we can say that the absence of this characteristic is an indication that we are not as fully developed as we ought to be.

But notice that James says that we must "let " or "allow" endurance to mature us. In other words, we are not to short-circuit the process. His wording is a command, putting us on guard against interrupting the process of maturity and interfering with God's design for our lives. And yet we still do that in so many ways. One way we short-circuit the process is to teach that Christians shouldn't have problems. Another is to insist that if we do have problems, God should solve them immediately. But, in fact, this text teaches that maturity takes time. It does not come in a sudden, blinding moment of ecstatic experience, but through steady, lifelong perseverance.

Another way to interrupt the process is to suggest that only mature and spiritual Christians with great faith can count on God for help. This verse teaches that God wants to test every Christian's faith, that is, to make it stronger, not through a miracle but through a trial. This verse, written by the half brother of Jesus Christ, runs full speed into those who shout that God wants Christians on easy street. The only way to Christian maturity is to endure trials. There are no shortcuts. And it is a lesson we learn every day of our lives. Alan Redpath adds this insightful word for us:

> There is nothing—no circumstance, no trouble, no testing—that can ever touch me until, first of all, it has gone past God and past Christ, right through to me. If it has come that far, it has come with great purpose, which I can not understand at the moment; but I refuse to become panicky, as I lift my eyes to Him and accept it as coming from the throne of God for some

great purpose of blessing to my own heart. So . . . no
sorrow will ever disturb me, no trial will ever alarm
me, no circumstance will cause me to fret, for I shall
rest in the joy of what my Lord is.[11]

As I reflect on nearly two decades of ministry, I recall
moments of great joy and happiness, times that I love to
replay. But I also find on the rewound video cartridge of
ministry periods of intense anguish which have assisted me
in growing spiritually. Oh, I didn't enjoy those periods. I
hated the pain. And I'm confident, given the option, I
wouldn't ask for second helpings of those courses, but I am
stronger and better for them.

When the bottom falls out of your life . . . and you wonder where God is in all of this, James urges you to cultivate
an attitude of joy, realizing God is in control. He pushes us
to acknowledge the fact that God does have a purpose in
our testing — He wants to develop within us the characteristic of endurance. Beyond that, he encourages us not to fight
the process, but to allow it to take its course so that in fact
we may develop spiritual maturity.

APPEALING FOR WISDOM

You may say, "But I still don't understand." Then look at
the final part of our response:

> But if any of you lacks wisdom, let him ask of God,
> who gives to all men generously and without reproach,
> and it will be given to him (v. 5).

This is God's offer of help to those of us facing trials we
don't understand. You may find yourself in such a web of
circumstances that there is no way it can make sense or
even begin to look like a stepping-stone to maturity. You
need help to see that. In a word, you need *wisdom.*

James talks here about the time of testing, before endurance has brought maturity, when we are still in the heat of

it. He assumes that we will face trials we won't understand, and will need wisdom to see and understand the nature and purpose of trials and know how to meet them. You see, wisdom is God-given insight into our human circumstances; it is the ability to see them from God's perspective. And all of us have that need. Someone has said, "When I panic, I run. When I run, I lose. When I lose, God waits. . . . But when I wait, He fights. When He fights, He wins. And when He wins, I learn."

God wants us to learn from our problems, to see them from His point of view, and He promises to give us that wisdom if we ask Him. James does not say *when* the answer will be given, only that it will be. Sometimes, it is not until much later that God reveals the reasons why He has allowed certain painful circumstances to enter our lives. And it is only then that we see the purpose. But the promise is clear: God will give the answer in His own way and at the time He chooses.

My God, my God, why hast Thou forsaken me?
Far from my deliverance are the words of my groaning.
O my God, I cry by day, but Thou dost not answer;
And by night, but I have no rest.
Yet Thou art holy.
O Thou who art enthroned upon the praises of Israel.
In Thee our fathers trusted;
They trusted, and Thou didst deliver them.
To Thee they cried out, and were delivered;
In Thee they trusted, and were not disappointed.

But I am a worm, and not a man,
A reproach of men, and despised by the people.
All who see me sneer at me;
They separate with the lip, they wag the head, saying,
"Commit yourself to the Lord, let Him deliver him;
Let Him rescue him, because He delights in him."

Yet Thou art He who didst bring me forth from the womb;
Thou didst make me trust when upon my mother's breasts.
Upon Thee I was cast from birth;
Thou hast been my God from my mother's womb.

Be not far from me, for trouble is near;
For there is none to help.
Many bulls have surrounded me;
Strong bulls of Bashan have encircled me.
They open wide their mouth at me,
As a ravening and a roaring lion.
I am poured out like water,
And all my bones are out of joint;
My heart is like wax;
It is melted within me.
My strength is dried up like a potsherd,
And my tongue cleaves to my jaws;
And Thou dost lay me in the dust of death.
For dogs have surrounded me;
A band of evildoers has encompassed me;
They pierced my hands and my feet.
I can count all my bones.

They look, they stare at me;
They divide my garments among them,
And for my clothing they cast lots.

But Thou, O Lord, be not far off;
O Thou my help, hasten to my assistance.
Deliver my soul from the sword,
My only life from the power of the dog.
Save me from the lion's mouth;
And from the horns of the wild oxen Thou dost answer me.

I will tell of Thy name to my brethren;
In the midst of the assembly I will praise Thee.
You who fear the Lord, praise Him;
All you descendants of Jacob, glorify Him,
And stand in awe of Him, all you descendants of Israel.
For He has not despised nor abhorred
the affliction of the afflicted;
Neither has He hidden His face from him;
But when he cried to Him for help, He heard.

From Thee comes my praise in the great assembly;
I shall pay my vows before those who fear Him.
The afflicted shall eat and be satisfied;
Those who seek Him will praise the Lord.
Let your heart live forever!
All the ends of the earth will remember and turn to the Lord,
And all the families of the nations will worship before Thee.
For the kingdom is the Lord's,
And He rules over the nations.
All the prosperous of the earth will eat and worship,
All those who go down to the dust will bow before Him,
Even he who cannot keep his soul alive.
Posterity will serve Him;
It will be told of the Lord to the coming generation.
They will come and will declare His righteousness
To a people who will be born, that He has performed it.
                                          Psalm 22

4
When Trouble Is Near

It's an old story, with a hundred variations, but I love it. Read it and let yourself smile for a moment.

A gentleman who was requesting sick leave needed to provide a written explanation to his insurance company and employer. This is what he wrote:

When I arrived at the construction site, I found that the hurricane had knocked off some bricks from around the top of the building. So, I rigged up a beam with a pulley at the top of the building and hoisted up a couple of barrels full of bricks. When I had fixed the damaged area, there were a lot of bricks left over. So, I went to the bottom of the building and began releasing the line. Unfortunately, the barrel of bricks was much heavier than I am — and before I knew what was happening, the barrel started coming down, jerking me up.

I decided to hang on since I was too far off the ground to jump, but halfway up I met the barrel of bricks coming down fast. I received a hard blow on my shoulder, I then continued to the top, banging my head against the beam and getting my fingers pinched and jammed in the pulley. Now then, when the barrel hit the ground hard, it burst its bottom, allowing the bricks to spill out. I was now heavier than the barrel. . . .

so, I started down again at high speed. Halfway down
I met the barrel coming up fast and received severe
injuries to my shins. When I hit the ground I landed
on the pile of spilled bricks, getting several painful
cuts and deep bruises. At this point, I must have lost
my presence of mind because I let go of my grip on
the line. The barrel came down fast — giving me another blow on my head and putting me in the hospital. I
respectfully request sick leave.[1]

About then, I might be more inclined to think about
retirement! Each of us understands, to some degree at
least, what it means to endure pain and suffering. For most
of us, however, pain does not produce a humorous accident
report. In fact, in the midst of our suffering, the last thing
we are thinking about is smiling or laughing. Psalm 22
reads like an accident report, but it's not funny. Yet, loom-
ing bright on the horizon of this psalm rises a perspective
of hope and praise. And so on the one hand, we find the
awful reality of painful experiences, and on the other hand,
the seemingly unreal experience of praise in spite of pain.
And what makes this even more complicated is that David's
pain was not just an isolated incident in his life. Already, in
chapter 2, we entered into his crucible of pain and felt the
pounding, the hammering. This psalm does nothing to dismantle that. In fact, it reminds us that trouble, suffering
and difficulties in our life never seem to go away, but,
rather, come to us in repetitive cycles.

The pattern of this psalm illustrates that. Verses 1-2 describe pain; while verses 3-5 spell relief. But then, verses 6-
8 describe more trouble, followed by more relief in verses
9-10. Rather than that being the end of the matter, trouble
once again assaults David in verses 11-18 with a positive
echo of praise and relief in the balance of the song. And
that is how our lives seem to go. Someone has said, "Life
can be counted on to provide all the pain that any of us
might need."

David was one of the first men of faith to record in detail

his suffering and then to recount his praise to God in the midst of it. Psalm 22 provides a pattern for sufferers to follow; it is a psalm for all seasons, especially seasons of suffering. And my friends, suffering is an inevitable season in our lives.

THE VARIETIES OF TROUBLE

So it was for David. Some awful experience of pain, physical and emotional, had assaulted him. And as was his habit, he sought relief from the unbearable agony in poetry ... and in his search for any words, any image of unbearable extremity and desperation by which to give expression to his pain. And there were different kinds of trouble that seemed to cycle his way.

● The first had a *spiritual* dimension to it.

My God, My God, why hast Thou forsaken me?
Far from my deliverance are the words of my groaning.
O my God, I cry by day, but Thou dost not answer;
And by night, but I have no rest (vv. 1-2).

David expressed the darkest mystery of his suffering—the sense of being forsaken by God. The word *forsaken* means "abandoned." But even more than that, the last part of verse 1 suggests not only abandonment, but a total lack of concern for David's plight. The Hebrew literally says, "Why are You so far from helping me? Why are you so far from the words of my groaning?"

Have you ever asked that? We all have, if not aloud, certainly down deep within our heart of hearts we have shouted these words ... wondering ... doubting. At such moments our experience seems to scream against our theology, doesn't it? David felt abandoned, not simply by friends or even family members now, but by the One on whom his very life depended ... his God. The One who promised never to leave His own had seemingly vanished from the scene. And when that is our story, we find ourselves harassed by doubt. We want to believe that God cares, but does He? You see, that's what doubt does to us. We waver between belief and disbelief. We seem to live in two minds. Perhaps Philip Yancey's book *Disappointment with God* accurately defines this feeling.

> I feel ashamed even to mention such an unanswered prayer. It seems petty and selfish, maybe even stupid, to pray for a car to start. But I have found that petty disappointments tend to accumulate over time, undermining my faith with a lava flow of doubt. I start to wonder whether God cares about everyday details— about me. I am tempted to pray less often, having concluded in advance that it won't matter. Or will it? My emotions and my faith waver. Once those doubts seep in, I am even less prepared for times of major crisis. A neighbor is dying of cancer; I pray diligently for her. But even as I pray, I wonder. Can God be trusted?[2]

When the pain of our trouble echoes through the megaphone of our experience, one of the first difficult encounters we face is spiritual in dimension.

● But there is another kind of trouble we've all met, one that is *interpersonal* in nature.

> But I am a worm, and not a man,
> A reproach of men, and despised by the people.
> All who see me sneer at me;
> They separate with the lip, they wag the head, saying,
> "commit yourself to the Lord; let Him deliver him;
> let Him rescue him, because He delights in him" (vv.
> 6-8).

Each word in this section is laced with mental and emotional suffering at the hands of others. Whereas David's problem with his God was expressed most powerfully in God's silence, the interpersonal problems arose out of the sarcastic way in which people spoke to and about David.

He had become a laughing-stock to many people, a disgrace, a reproach. And so they would lift their heads, look down their noses at David, and "sneer" at him. That verb in verse 7 comes from a root that means "to stammer, or to stutter," and it suggests not a one-time attack but a constant harangue. And one of they ways they did that was by "separating the lip." That's a poetic way of saying that they opened their mouths wide and insulted David.

It gets to you when people laugh at your pain, at your extremity. When they make light of your trouble, as they did David's, that hurts. You feel absolutely isolated. David certainly did.

Be not far from me, for trouble is near;
For there is none to help (v. 11).

There is even a hint to this in the title of the psalm. Notice what it says, "For the choir director; upon aijeleth." In the margin of your Bible *aijeleth* may be translated, "the hind of the morning." The word *hind* describes a lonely deer, cut off from the rest of its herd at dawn, standing on a cliff gazing into the distance in the hope of discovering its friends. That's how you feel when people laugh at your pain. In such moments, it is difficult, if not impossible, to describe your anguish. So it seemed to David. In their scorn they had the audacity to say to David:

Commit yourself to the Lord; let Him deliver him;
Let Him rescue him, because He delights in him
(v. 8).

They were laughing at what was left of David's faith, taunting him, reopening his wounds by reminding him sarcastically that he could always trust his God to help him. Such taunts are hard to answer. They seem to drive the wedge deeper between our doubts and our faith. And the more we struggle in that arena, the worse we feel.

• David began to show signs of the struggle in *physical* troubles.

Be not far from me, for trouble is near;
For there is none to help. . . .
I am poured out like water,
And all my bones are out of joint;
My heart is like wax;
It is melted within me.
My strength is dried up like a potsherd,
And my tongue cleaves to my jaws;
And Thou dost lay me in the dust of death.
For dogs have surrounded me;
A band of evildoers has encompassed me;
They pierced my hands and my feet.
I can count all my bones.
They look, they stare at me;
They divide my garments among them,
And for my clothing they cast lots (vv. 11, 14-18).

In verse 11, the verb *to help* literally means "someone who builds walls." And David felt as if there was nobody who cared enough to help build a wall of support or protection around him. When we find ourselves mired in a place like that, it only makes our physical problems worse. Part of the suffering David was undergoing at this time was physical in nature, and his feelings of isolation only intensified his pain.

We shouldn't be surprised. Health studies show that single, widowed, and divorced people are far likelier prey to disease than married people. Some authorities argue that social isolation brings emotional and then physical deterioration. There is a medical basis for our need to form human relationships. If we fail to fulfill that need, our health is in peril.

In verses 14 and 15, David was describing a serious health problem. He felt completely washed out and as if all his bones were disjointed. He was physically, emotionally and mentally exhausted. He was completely spent, devastated, so tired that he wondered if he would ever feel rested again.

And what made it worse was that his enemies were, even in his moment of pain, figuring ways to cash in on his potential demise. David was sick but not dead. But they were dividing up his possessions as if he were already gone.

That reminds me of the five-year-old boy who had an incredible interest in motorcycles. Whenever he saw one he would let out a howl of joy, accompanied by animated remarks, "Look at that! Look at that! I'm going to get a motorcycle someday." His father's answer was always the same, "Not so long as I'm alive, you won't." One day, while the boy was talking to his friend, a brand new bike zoomed by. He excitedly pointed it out to the boy and said, "Look at that! Look at that! I'm getting one of those—*as soon as my dad dies.*"

That's how people were treating David's pain. And no matter how you slice that, you draw blood. Pain is like that. Its interruption in our lives disrupts and reshapes. It intercepts our hopes and plans; it rearranges our dreams. It always leaves a mark. Suffering shakes and stuns us. And in our state of shock we are inclined to label the entire experience as useless, without purpose, without rationale. We all feel that pull, especially when others laugh at our pain, when they ridicule our faith in God, when they make us feel inferior because we still believe. And we wonder.

THE GIFTS OF GOD

Life can be like that—not just as advertised, not what we came to see. And we wonder about its value. Margaret Clarkson, a gifted hymnwriter who has wrestled with deep agonies of heart and body has a good word for us.

> Pain is pain and sorrow is sorrow. It hurts. It limits. It impoverishes. It isolates. It restrains. It works devastation deep within the personality. It circumscribes in a thousand different ways. There is nothing good about it. *But the gifts God can give with it* are the richest the human spirit can know.[3]

And that is where David would have us concentrate. Not simply on the trouble in his life, but also on the *relief* that he found was available to him. It comes in four packages and they all wrap around the person and character of His God.

  • God's Holiness and Faithfulness.

Yet Thou art holy,
O Thou who art enthroned upon the praises of Israel.
In Thee our fathers trusted;
They trusted, and Thou didst deliver them.
To Thee they cried out, and were delivered;
In Thee they trusted, and were not disappointed
(vv. 3-5).

In the midst of trouble, David went for the highest ground of all: the holiness of God. That is significant, because in the Bible, holiness is the most frequently mentioned attribute of God. Whenever an individual in the Bible approached God, he was overwhelmed, first of all, not with a sense of God's love but with a sense of His holiness. God's holiness represents the fact that He is separate from us and exalted over us. And although David may have felt that God was silent, he believed that his God was still there, exalted over Him. But that does not suggest that God was unapproachable, so far removed that He could not be trusted.

In verses 4 and 5, David looked back to other times of history and to other men's experiences of help and found anchored in those histories a testimony to the faithfulness of God. In fact, it was God's past record that gave David hope and offers us hope in our darkest moments. Our confidence today is grounded on what God has done in the past. When we are in the tidal wave of trouble, it is essential to look back at our own lives and the lives of others who have gone before and to find hope in those experiences. As hopeless as our present pain makes our situations appear, God's track record of holiness and faithfulness stands without argument. And it is from that record, that we must draw our hope.

The late Joe Bayly understood that hope. He and his wife lost three sons. In the midst of some of that he penned this word of hope:

> I find it hard, Lord, agonizing hard to stand here looking through the glass at this my infant son. What suffering is in this world to go through, pain of birth and pain of knife within the day.
>
> What suffering is in the world this never ending pain parade from birth to death. He moves a bit. Not much. How could an infant stuffed with tubes cut sewed and bandaged move more than that? Some day he'll shout and run a race, roll down a grassy hill and ice skate on a frosty night like this. He'll sing and laugh. I know he will Lord.
>
> But if not, if You should take him home to Your home, help me then remember how Your Son suffered and You stood by watching, agonizing, watching, waiting to bring all suffering to an end forever on a day yet to be. Look, Lord, he sleeps. I must go now. Thank You for staying nearer than oxygen, than dripping plasma to my son. Please be that near to mother, sister, brothers and to me.[4]

● God's Care.

> Yet Thou art He who didst bring me forth from the womb;
> Thou didst make me trust when upon my mother's breasts.
> Upon Thee I was cast from birth;
> Thou hast been my God from my mother's womb.
> For He has not despised nor abhorred the affliction of the afflicted;
> Neither has He hidden His face from him;
> But when he cried to Him for help, He heard (vv. 9-10, 24).

To confront the ridicule and scorn of others, David clung

to what he had left, to what he knew, deep inside, for certain. And despite his doubts . . . despite his wonderings, his questions, despite all that, deep down inside the combat zone of his soul *he was confident of God's care in his own life.*

You see, it is one thing to examine the lives of others over time and see the thread of God's faithfulness; it is quite another to examine your own life. Looking at others can still keep you distant, aloof, cold, unmoved. But looking honestly into your own experiences forces either an incredible denial of God's involvement in your life or an increasing gratitude for His gracious care. David then recalled how from his birth God had preserved and protected him. God was with him personally, right from his birth. There had never been a moment throughout his existence when God was not with him and this now was his confidence, his relief. David was dwelling on God's personal, lifelong care, for God was no casual acquaintance. Even when his enemies were tightening the screws and stretching the rack, David knew that he was really in God's hands, as he always had been.

And what's more, according to verse 24 God did not take his suffering lightly, or write him off as unworthy of care.

For He has not despised nor abhorred the affliction of
the afflicted;
Neither has He hidden His face from him;
But when he cried to Him for help, He heard (v. 24).

One bold message that leaps off the pages of this ancient hymnbook is that you can say anything to God. Throw at Him your grief, your anger, your doubt, your bitterness, your betrayal, your disappointment, your pain — He can absorb them all. . . . and He will, without disdain. One writer expressed it this way:

Have you ever pulled the petals from a flower, saying to yourself, "He loves me, he loves me not"? And the last petal said, "Not." It's a foolish little love game —

but I do feel rather bad when it ends with "Not." With God it never ends that way! Every petal says to me, "He loves me, He loves me!" His love is always, and forever, and now — but never *not.*[5]

• God's Sovereignty. The holiness and faithfulness of God, linked to His care, brought a measure of relief to David. But so did his understanding of the sovereignty of his God.

> For the kingdom is the Lord's,
> And He rules over the nations.
> All the prosperous of the earth will eat and worship,
> All those who go down to the dust will bow before Him,
> Even he who cannot keep his soul alive.
> Posterity will serve Him;
> It will be told of the Lord to the coming generation.
> They will come and will declare His righteousness
> To a people who will be born, that He has performed it (vv. 28-31).

In the final sense, these verses look beyond the moment that David encircled to a time yet in the future when God in Christ will rule the universe. But within that span is the unchanging truth that God is king and controls the affairs of mankind. Therefore, the particular events in our lives that we call "distress, trouble, pain, and tragedy" must be seen in this larger perspective of God's sovereignty. The text is very clear — God's kingdom sovereignty embraces those who do well in this life and those whose lives crumble at the seams. That's the heartbeat of verse 29. But verses 30 and 31 include the unborn generations that follow.

Several years ago now, a then unknown rabbi, Harold Kushner, published his first book, *When Bad Things Happen to Good People*. It instantly became a best-seller. The book deals with a familiar theme: how can a loving God allow such terrible suffering in the world? It's an age-old question. Drawing from his own experience — his son died

at age fourteen of a tragic illness — Kushner answered that
God is indeed all-loving, but not all-powerful; the bad
things which happen are simply out of His control. He
writes, "I can worship a God who hates suffering but cannot eliminate it, more easily than I can worship a God who
chooses to make children suffer and die."

People consumed the book with a frenzy. But as Chuck
Colson so aptly observes, "The god Kushner writes about is
neither omnipotent nor sovereign, and is, therefore, not the
Creator God . . . not the all-powerful God revealed in
the . . . Bible."[6]

Dr. Vernon Grounds, former president of Denver Seminary and a compassionate and thoughtful man, wrote this in
a letter:

> One thing which impresses me more and more is the
> bewildering tragedy of human life. As I counsel with
> emotionally broken individuals and as I observe the
> pain, injustice and frustration in the world, I cling
> tenaciously to my conviction that God, infinitely wise
> and loving, is *sovereign.* And the empty tomb demon-
> strates that out of the worst which can take place, He
> is able to bring forth His own glorious best. Yet I
> understand the experience of Carroll E. Simcox who,
> in his *The Eternal You,* confesses that one day he
> heard God saying, "I wish you'd leave all this reconcil-
> ing of things to Me, since you are so hopelessly un-
> equipped for it, and that you would use whatever in-
> fluence you have with your fellow fussers and worriers
> to do likewise. I know what I'm doing. I'll go over it
> with you when you get home." Like Simcox, I have
> quit worrying and fussing over the intractable problem
> of evil, confident that God's explanation will complete-
> ly satisfy my mind and heart.[7]

● God's Worthiness. That is where David stood and it
brought him finally to the last aspect of relief, the worth
and worship of his God.

I will tell of Thy name to my brethren;

In the midst of the assembly I will praise Thee.
You who fear the Lord, praise Him;
All you descendants of Jacob, glorify Him,
And stand in awe of Him, all you descendants of
Israel.
For He has not despised nor abhorred the affliction of
the afflicted;
Neither has He hidden His face from him;
But when he cried to Him for help, He heard.
From Thee comes my praise in the great assembly;
I shall pay my vows before those who fear Him
(vv. 22-25).

In the midst of his anguish, David looked forward and upward. He knew who God is, what He is like and what He can do. And so he not only worshiped his God, but invited his friends to join the celebration. The word *praise* used in these verses means "boasting in God's character and His works." *Glorifying* God is "magnifying Him by speaking of what He has done for me personally." *Standing in awe* of God is "being overcome by reverence before His power and His might."

That is true worship, when our hearts and minds are focused on God, not on ourselves. And yet, isn't much of our evaluation of "worship" based on how we feel about the church service? Sure it is. But that means our worship is focused more on the worshiper than on the One worshiped. Years ago, William Temple described true worship in this way:

For worship is the submission of all our nature to God. It is the quickening of conscience by His *holiness;* the nourishment of mind with His *truth;* the purifying of imagination by His *beauty;* the opening of the heart to His *love;* the surrender of our will to His *purpose* — and all of this gathered up in *adoration,* the most self-less emotion of which our nature is capable and, therefore, the chief remedy for that self-centeredness which is our original sin and the source of all actual sin.[8]

There is one other part to this worship that we must not miss. Lying beneath David's history in this psalm, there is another Person to whom the words apply. It is clear, from the words of Jesus on the cross — "My God, My God, why hast Thou forsaken Me?" that He identified His own loneliness and suffering with David's. It is not without reason that this psalm has been called the "Fifth Gospel" account of the crucifixion. Verse 16 says, "They pierced my hands and my feet . . . and for my clothing they cast lots." My friends, the sufferer of Psalm 22 is not only David; it is also the God-Man experiencing the terror of mortality in the absence of God the Father, and in the presence of His enemies. On the cross, we see Jesus Christ Himself entering into and participating in the terror of pain. He identified with the suffering we endure, and with our dying. But because He has been through it, He can offer to us His comfort and His love. *The Amplified Bible,* in expressing the words of the writer of the Book of Hebrews puts it to us this way:

> For we do not have a high priest who is unable to sympathize and have a fellow feeling with our weaknesses and infirmities, but One who has been tempted in every respect as we are, yet without sinning. Let us then fearlessly and confidently and boldly draw near to the throne of grace — the throne of God's unmerited favor, that we may receive mercy and find grace to help in good times for every need — appropriate help and well-timed help, coming just when we need it (4:15-16).

You are loved by Him and you are valuable to Him!

The Lord is my light and my salvation;
Whom shall I fear?
The Lord is the defense of my life;
Whom shall I dread?
When evildoers came upon me to devour my flesh,
My adversaries and my enemies,
they stumbled and fell.
Though a host encamp against me,
My heart will not fear;
Though war arise against me,
In spite of this I shall be confident.

One thing I have asked from the Lord,
that I shall seek;
That I may dwell in the house of the Lord
all the days of my life,
To behold the beauty of the Lord,
And to meditate in His temple.
For in the day of trouble He will conceal me
in His tabernacle;
In the secret place of His tent He will hide me;
He will lift me up on a rock.
And now my head will be lifted up above
my enemies around me;
And I will offer in His tent sacrifices
with shouts of joy;
I will sing, yes, I will sing praises to the Lord.

Hear, O Lord, when I cry with my voice,
And be gracious to me and answer me.
When Thou didst say, "Seek My face,"
my heart said to Thee,
"Thy face, O Lord, I shall seek."
Do not hide Thy face from me,
Do not turn Thy servant away in anger;
Thou hast been my help;
Do not abandon me nor forsake me,
O God of my salvation!
For my father and my mother have forsaken me,
But the Lord will take me up.

Teach me Thy way, O Lord,
And lead me in a level path,
Because of my foes.
Do not deliver me over to the
desire of my adversaries;
For false witnesses have risen against me,
And such as breathe out violence.

I would have despaired unless I had believed that
I would see the goodness of the Lord
In the land of the living.
Wait for the Lord;
Be strong, and let your heart take courage;
Yes, wait for the Lord.

Psalm 27

5
Running Scared

I f you have ever been gripped in a stranglehold of fear, you will never forget this incident that happened in June of 1980. If you have ever run for your life; you will find yourself running in this story. It began with one terror-filled statement: *"Don't shoot him in the head!"*

With that, Peggy Hunter came fully alive in the tent. She grabbed her daughter, Jennifer, and they fled for their lives into the Cleveland National Forest in California. It was June 16, and for the next two weeks they remained on the run. They ate berries, and they covered themselves with dirt for warmth at night.

Every time they heard the pursuing men, they fled faster and further. After two weeks, they came to a clearing. Peggy Hunter stumbled out into the highway in her tattered clothes; glassy-eyed and with her twelve-year-old daughter — who was now completely naked, she hailed a passing car. That ended a two-week search for these two missing persons who were presumed dead.

The search party that had looked desperately for them was driven on by the conviction that this mother and daughter had been kidnapped by a motorcycle gang camping in the park. But that was not the case. In fact, it had all started with a shot fired at a raccoon, and the statement,

"Don't shoot him in the head!"

Everyone was embarrassed; everyone was exhausted; everyone was thankful. But everyone who read the article took a new look at the fear in his or her own life.

What is it that causes us to flee for our lives when the danger isn't real? What is it that causes us to assume that the voices we hear are pursuing us, not just looking for us? What is that prompts us to believe that we are in mortal danger every day? *Fear.* And we all live with it.[1]

In 1935, T.S. Eliot expressed his generation's fears in his dramatic play, *Murder in the Cathedral.* "We have seen the young man mutilated, the torn girl trembling by the mill-stream. And meanwhile we have gone on living . . . we have all had *our private terror . . .* "[2]

In discussing our current society, Dr. Willard Gaylin slices through the self-imposed layers of protection we wear, and exposes our real vulnerability:

> We have constructed a civilization that, for the most part, protects us from the onslaught of other life forms or the uncivilized within our species. We have invented the law to institutionalize our security and our values. We resist even the elements. And still we see ourselves *endangered.* What threatens this triumphant species, "Homo sapiens," during a period in which he has fulfilled the biblical prophecy of his supremacy over the "fowls of the air and the beasts of the earth, and the fishes of the sea?" *What frightens us so? We are out of the jungle and we still do not feel safe![3]*

David, the ancient king of Israel, understood fear. Even though he was a rugged man who could survive alone in the rough terrain of the land of Judah, even though he was strong enough to kill a lion and courageous enough to confront and defeat Goliath, David still knew fear. In Psalm 27:1 he asks two related questions that show us this:

> The Lord is my light and my salvation;
> Whom shall I fear?

The Lord is the defense of my life;
Whom shall I dread? (v. 1)

Now, please understand what David is *not* saying. He is
not asking, "Whom shall I begin to be afraid of in the
future . . . say, tomorrow or next week?" He is not suggesting that he has not known fear, or that fear is foreign to
him. Rather, he is asking, *"Who will I continue to fear?*
Who will I continue to run from? Who will I allow to so
control my life that I live a life of dread? How long will I
let the statement, 'Don't shoot him in the head,' drive me?"

KNOWING GOD

Fear was something David understood, but it was also
something he had an answer for. In fact, the way he asked
these questions indicated that he no longer was controlled
by his fears, or by those people who would incite fear
within him. The reason was that he had a *personal relationship* with his God. "The Lord is my light and my salvation."
This is the only time in the Old Testament that the term
light is applied directly to the Lord God. Its appearance is
significant because such light refers to the *knowability of
God.* Just as it is the nature of light to make things visible,
so too, God must make Himself known. Light then is used
to picture God making Himself known in salvation. (That is
why Jesus Christ could declare that He is the light of the
world, and that if you have seen Him you have seen God.
Jesus Christ is the ultimate visible declaration of God. God
the Father made Himself completely known through Christ.)
David was assuring himself that God—pictured as light—
makes Himself known in salvation.

But you'll notice that David also declared that God was
the "defense" of his life. The word is used figuratively of
God as a person of refuge. God was the stronghold of David's life. It was in the person and character of God that

David found security and release from fear. David made a point of saying that God is light . . . salvation . . . and defense. He did not say that God *gives* those things. In other words, David's emphasis was on *who God is*. To David, He was a very personal, ever-present friend, not some impersonal, abstract, theological Being who hid Himself above the clouds. He was David's companion, and David found release from fear in the presence of God.

Betsie ten Boom, who died during her imprisonment in World War II, knew only too well that the prison she was in was hell on earth, but she was never overwhelmed by the darkness around her. She was so certain that the light of God and His gospel was greater than the darkness of the enemy that she could say to her sister, Corrie:

> The most important part of our task will be to tell everyone who will listen that Jesus is the only answer to the problems that are disturbing the hearts of men and nations. We shall have the right to speak because we can tell from our experience that His light is more powerful than the deepest darkness. . . . How wonderful that the reality of His presence is greater than the reality of the hell around us.[4]

David understood that because he understood his God. The word that He chose for God, translated in verse 1 as "the Lord," is the Hebrew term *YHWH* or *Jehovah*. It means "I am that I am." That is to say, "I am really and truly present in your life, ready to help and act, just as I always have been."

That is why He was David's light and salvation. Is He yours? Do you live in the presence of God? Or, is He only Someone you think is there? Richard Halverson puts our proper perspective in words when he prays:

> Almighty God, we respond to Thee in many different ways.
> Some deny Thee altogether. Others acknowledge Thee but ignore Thee.

Some take Thee seriously. Others tip the hat to Thee occasionally.
Some worship and adore Thee. Others could not care less.
Some love Thee. Others fear Thee.
Some know Thee. Others feel Thou art beyond knowing.
Some see Thee as a living reality, others as an impersonal force.

But whatever our attitude, Father in heaven, rarely do we think of Thee as practical or relevant to our personal or corporate problems. Help us understand that Thou art a God who cares — who seeks us — who longs for us. Help us see that Thou art the source of all wisdom and power — that Thou art an infinite resource available to meet our needs.

Forgive our indifference and grant us grace to call upon Thee, however great or small our problems.

Help us to see in the cross the measure of Thy love, Thy nearness, Thy availability.[5]

EXPERIENCING PAIN

You may be thinking, "Look, that's great. I'm glad for David. But if you only knew my situation, you'd sing a different tune. You don't understand my circumstances." Well, let's look at some of the things David faced and see if you relate to them.

When evildoers came upon me to devour my flesh,
My adversaries and my enemies, they stumbled and fell.
Though a host encamp against me,
My heart will not fear;
Though war arise against me,
In spite of this I shall be confident (vv. 2-3)

David was harried, hunted and hounded by people who didn't like him. Verse 2 reads, "*When* evildoers came upon me . . . " not, "*If* they came upon me." The term *evildoers* describes their intent; it means "those who produce hurt in someone's life." Now, they could have chosen any number of ways to do that, but they selected the most popular and effective way—they slandered and lied about David. That is what the phrase "to devour my flesh" refers to in verse 3, and links to others who are described in verse 12 as "false witnesses." The people were prepared to stand in court and commit perjury just so they could call David a liar. This is what David was wrestling with, but he didn't know *when* or *where* it would happen, and that uncertainty produces fear. You know people are gunning for you, but you can't see the guns. But still you keep hearing, "Don't shoot him in the head!"

It wasn't that long ago that this kind of fear corralled my life. It got so bad that I dreaded running into the six or seven men in the church who were gunning for me. Oh sure, I'd been warned, but I didn't think it would really happen to me. It did. I dreaded their phone calls, the verbal beatings, their closed-door meetings to discuss my inadequacies. I kept thinking, "I hear shots!"

Like you, like me, David experienced pain that was close up and personal. People ripped at him, tore at him, and used him. People who were close to him tried to take advantage of him. At other times, the problems confronting him seemed as if a war was breaking over his head. How could that be?

What we must understand is that David, at this moment in his life, had been run off his throne by his son Absalom. As a result, David was in hiding and in desperate circumstances. He had been forced to set up a government in exile and organize his loyal forces to meet the expected attack of his own son.

Absalom, in the meantime, gathered all the outstanding young men to his cause. He publicly disgraced his father by lying about him and even now was preparing a great army to finish off his father. To make it even worse, it appears from verse 10 that David's own parents wrote him off, "For my father and my mother have forsaken me . . . " Think about that! Humiliated, outgunned and heavily outnumbered, David knew fear, because he had no idea what lay ahead of him . . . just like some of you.

Some wives wonder if they are next in line to be traded in for a new and younger model, as many of their friends have been. Young people sit in their rooms alone with the stereo blasting, worrying whether their parents will stay together. Career persons are uncertain in their jobs; others wonder if they will ever be able to keep up with the ongoing training that seems necessary. Senior citizens are fearful of being unable to afford the luxury of staying alive. Singles fear the icy tentacles of loneliness that are never far away. Our fear of what lies in wait has been expressed in an intense and heartbroken way by Alan Paton.

> I see my son is wearing long trousers, I tremble at this;
> I see he goes forward confidently, he does not know so fully his own gentleness.
> Go forward, eager and reverent child, see here I begin to take my hands away from you,
> (but) I shall see you walk careless on the edges of the precipice, but if you wish you shall hear no word come out of me.
> My whole soul will be sick with apprehension, but I shall not disobey you.
> Life sees you coming, she sees you come with assurance toward her.
> She lies in wait for you, she cannot but hurt you;
> Go forward, go forward, I hold the bandages and ointments ready.[6]

GODLY CONFIDENCE

David understood the hurts of life . . . the fear . . . like you do. But still he declared, "The Lord is my light and my salvation." David had an abiding confidence in his God. The verb in verse 3 translated as "shall be confident" expresses a present tense reality in David's life. It comes from a word which means "to throw yourself down on the ground, to lie with your face in the dirt." It is the posture of one who is confident not in himself, but in his God. It is the picture of ultimate trust. Self-sufficiency is not a mark of greatness. The truly great person is very aware of his limitations. It is the arrogant, stubborn person who is self-sufficient; he is unconscious of, or unwilling to admit to, his limitations and is really insensitive to his dependence upon others or God. Rather than admit dependence, the little person bluffs his way through, and when he fails, blames circumstances or others. Having then convinced himself that someone or something else is to blame, he loses one more opportunity to know himself. Becoming more entrenched in his own self-delusion, he plows ahead in false self-confidence.

That was not David's posture. He was on his face before the God of his salvation, and he was confident.

> For in the day of trouble He will conceal me in his tabernacle;
> In the secret place of His tent He will hide me;
> He will lift me up on a rock (v. 5)

The word *tabernacle* describes a place of temporary shelter, and the word *tent* refers to God's presence in our life. David was describing the times in his life *when he was not taken out of the battle,* the times when the hurts, the struggles, and the pressures of life did not go away, but cut him deeply. And although God did not remove him from the pain, yet, somehow by His spiritual presence, God covered David's heart of hearts in the midst of the pain. And sometimes, that's all we have. We too experience what David did — there is no change in our circumstances; yet God, in His grace, marvelously protects us and grants us peace in the midst of our turmoil. With Charles Haddon Spurgeon, we would say, "When we cannot trace God's hand, we can trust God's heart." That is where David rested his confidence.

But there are other times when God offers a different kind of help. Look at the last part of verse 5, " . . . He will lift me up on a rock." Sometimes God sets us on a rock; that is, we find ourselves removed by His hand from the difficult circumstance. God sovereignly moves in and takes care of things . . . and we are left with our mouths hanging open, wondering how it all came together. And in those times, and for these reasons, we can have confidence in Him.

You see, regardless of our circumstances, regardless whether God comforts us in them or removes them from us, there is one thing that never changes, if we know Him and trust Him. That one certain thing is in verse 10, "The Lord will take me up." This literally means, "The Lord will adopt me." David's parents, for some unexplained reason, said, "That's it . . . we don't want him anymore." We don't know for sure, but perhaps the conflict with Absalom, their grandson, prompted this reaction. That would not be uncommon . . . taking sides in family conflicts. We're not sure. But needless to say, David needed this reminder from his God. . . . "David, I am still your Father in heaven. . . . I have adopted you." That is a tremendous truth for us to grasp. Dr. J.I. Packer reflects on it in this way:

> What is a Christian? The question can be answered in many ways, but the richest answer I know is that a Christian is one who has God for his Father . . . The revelation to the believer that God is his Father is in a sense the climax of the Bible. If you want to judge how well a person understands Christianity, find out how much he makes of the thought of being God's child, and having God as his Father. If this is not the thought that prompts and controls his worship and prayers and his whole outlook on life, it means that he does not understand Christianity very well at all. Father is the Christian name for God.[7]

David understood that. And when his heart skipped a beat with fear, when he felt like the guns of his enemies were pointing at his head, when he was on the run for his life, his confidence, his trust was in his Heavenly Father.

Today, Lord
I have an unshakable conviction
A positive resolute assurance
That what You have spoken
Is unalterably true.

But today, Lord
My sick body feels stronger
And the stomping pain quietly subsides. . . .
Tomorrow. . . .

And then tomorrow
If I must struggle again
With aching exhaustion
With twisting pain
Until I am breathless
Until I am utterly spent
Until fear eclipses the last vestige of hope
Then, Lord
Then grant me the enabling grace
To believe without feeling
To know without seeing
To clasp Your invisible hand
And wait with invincible trust
for the morning.[8]

WORSHIP AND OBEDIENCE

We can worship when our confidence is in our Father in heaven. But it won't be if our spiritual heartbeat is wavering. David's heartbeat slowed spiritually at times. But here it was properly focused on *worshiping* His God.

One thing I have asked from the lord, that I shall seek:

That I may dwell in the house of the Lord all the days
of my life,
To behold the beauty of the Lord.
And to meditate in His temple.

And now my head will be lifted up above my enemies
around me;
And I will offer in His tent sacrifices with shouts of
joy;
I will sing, yes, I will sing praises to the Lord.

When Thou didst say, "Seek My face," my heart said
to Thee, "Thy face, O Lord, I shall seek" (vv. 4, 6, 8).

David was reiterating the theme he had introduced in
verse 1. He wanted to be at home in the presence of God.
To be in God's presence is to have an attitude of appreciation and delight in the goodness of God. And David was
saying, "The place I want to be . . . the place where I know
I belong . . . is face to face with God, in His presence."

The staggering part of David's desire is that according to
verse 4, he asked that he might be blessed with this all the
days of his life. David said, in effect, "My desire is not
going to fade with time; it is not something that I feel now
and again, on religious holidays. This is an everyday, all the
days of my life, forever kind of longing."

In expressing that longing, he concentrated again on
God's character. He wanted "to behold the beauty of the
Lord," that is, all that God consists of in His glory. What a
great place to be!

When we are intimidated, when we lack confidence, we
are more conscious of the person attacking us than we are
of the Lord. And so when we step into a scene that is
frightening, we must consciously see ourselves in God's
presence, meditating upon Him, beholding His glory and
saying to Him, "Right now, Lord, I have nothing to draw
upon . . . nothing . . . except You."

When our hearts flow in that direction, we become

thankful people. David did. In verse 6, the phrase "shouts
of joy" is a strong expression for sacrifices of jubilant
thanksgiving. David was going to offer sacrifices in which
gratitude would play a prominent role. . . . and he would
sing songs of thanksgiving to his God.

Do you see how it works? When we are afraid of the
future, we remember who our light and salvation really is.
When people harass us, when they make it their goal in life
to hurt us verbally, we fall on our face before our God and
concentrate on who He is . . . on His beauty and His glory.
We make it our desire to worship Him, and when we do,
He prompts us to offer up "shouts of joy" and thanksgiving.
As that occurs, something else becomes crucial to us . . . our
obedience to our God.

> Teach me Thy way, O Lord,
> And lead me in a level path,
> Because of my foes (v. 11).

David knew that if he stumbled into the alleyway of sin,
it would dishonor God. He knew that a disobedient life is a
rocky road, not a level one, so he prayed to be led in the
way of God, to have the strength of character to obey God's
commands. A worshiping heart moves in that direction.

But that is so tough! Especially when you're afraid, when
you're not sure which end is up, and you are desperately
trying to work things out. Then it is most difficult to obey.
Max Lucado expresses our struggle in this imaginative way:

> It's as if there were a miniature receptionist in our
> brain instructed to intercept all warnings and file them
> in appropriate files. Can you imagine the scene?
>
> "Hello. Screening department. May I help you?"
>
> "Yes. This is the safety spectrum. I'm calling to ad-
> vise Mr. Lucado that he is driving too fast."
>
> "I'm sorry. Mr. Lucado left instructions that that
> particular warning was for the 'other guy' who isn't as
> experienced on highways."
>
> Or perhaps, "This is Mr. Lucado's conscience calling."

"I'm sorry, Mr. Lucado left word that he is having his horizon expanded and doesn't plan to return your call."

Or, "This is the Conviction Section. I need to arrange for Mr. Lucado to read the book of James within the next twenty-four hours. There are a couple of things he needs to remember."

"Let me check his schedule . . . hmmm. The next time Mr. Lucado is free to read the Bible is next month. However, he does have several golf games scheduled. Is there any way you can talk to him on the golf course?"

Even, "This is Mr. Lucado's faith calling to remind him — hello? Hello? That's strange, I've been disconnected."[9]

Fearful hearts struggle with obedience. Worshiping hearts struggle less.

THE GOODNESS OF GOD

Where does all of this lead us? To the same place it led David.

> I would have despaired unless I had believed that
> I would see the goodness of the Lord
> In the land of the living (v. 13).

In your Bible the first several words of this verse, "I would have despaired," or "I had fainted," may be in italics. That means they have been added by the translators to help us understand the verse. David simply said, "Unless I had believed that I would see the goodness of the Lord in the land of the living . . . " It is not a sentence at all, but a cry which is almost a groan. David did not finish it, but left it for us to complete in our own fearful circumstances.

Some of us would cry, "I would have turned to drugs and alcohol, unless I had believed." Still others would cry, "Unless I had believed that God was in control, that His good

must triumph—regardless of how desperately afraid I am. . . .
unless I held that confidence, I would have given up long
ago, I would have lost my life in cynicism, and sin." Still
others would cry, "Unless I had believed in God's goodness, I would have walked away from this marriage a long
time ago." We would all have our own painful cries.

I've been there, when the machine guns wouldn't stop.
When I struggled the most with this a number of years ago,
I remember sitting at my desk and investigating the addresses of the medical schools I had once applied to before
my seminary years. I wanted to go back to medical school
and graduate and join my father in his practice. I cried,
"Unless I had believed that God was in control, that His
good must triumph, I would have quit the ministry." I
didn't . . . because of my belief.

David had his confidence in God's sovereignty to fall
back on. And sometimes that is all there is. There are frankly days when fear climbs aboard my life—uninvited, unwel-
come—and claws for attention. And in those moments,
sometimes there is nothing else that I can cling to but an
abiding trust in the goodness of God. In those times, we
must cry from the bottom of our hearts the words of David:

> Wait for the Lord;
> Be strong and let your heart take courage;
> Yes, wait for the Lord (v. 14).

Charles Haddon Spurgeon wrote of this verse, "Wait at
His door with prayer; wait at His feet with humility; wait at
His table with service; wait at His window with expectancy."

The verb *wait* describes the making of a strong, powerful
rope by twisting, weaving and stretching many strands of
thread together. It carries the idea of our twisting and
weaving ourselves so tightly around the Lord God that our
weaknesses and frail characteristics begin, in time, to be
replaced by His strength and His power. Sometimes, there
is nothing more to do.

I met Dave for the first time in 1980. He was tall and

handsome, in his mid-thirties, with a lovely wife and family. He served as an elder in the church I came to pastor. I didn't know then that several years before he had been operated on for cancer of the lung. Little did I know that two years later Patricia and I would wait with his wife for ten hours while surgery was again performed on Dave, this time for brain cancer. Just last year, another operation was performed in an attempt to remove three more tumors in his brain.

As I talked long distance to his dear wife, she said that Dave had told her before and even after the surgery the same thing he always told me, "I'm in the hands of the Lord . . . and He is good."

What a perspective! What a God!

Give ear to my prayer, O God;
And do not hide Thyself from my supplication.
Give heed to me, and answer me;
I am restless in my complaint and am surely distracted,
Because of the voice of the enemy,
Because of the pressure of the wicked;
For they bring down trouble upon me,
And in anger they bear a grudge against me.

My heart is in anguish within me,
And the terrors of death have fallen upon me.
Fear and trembling come upon me;
And horror has overwhelmed me.
And I said, "O that I had wings like a dove!
I would fly away and be at rest.
"Behold, I would wander far away,
I would lodge in the wilderness.
I would hasten to my place of refuge.
From the stormy winds and tempest."

Confuse, O Lord, divide their tongues,
For I have seen violence and strife in the city.
Day and night they go around her upon her walls;
And iniquity and mischief are in her midst.
Destruction is in her midst;
Oppression and deceit do not depart from her streets.

For it is not an enemy who reproaches me,
Then I could bear it;
Nor is it one who hates me who has exalted himself against me,
Then I could hide myself from him.
But it is you, a man my equal,
My companion and my familiar friend.
We who had sweet fellowship together,
Walked in the house of God in the throng.
Let death come deceitfully upon them;
Let them go down alive to Sheol,
For evil is in their dwelling, in their midst.

As for me, I shall call upon God,
And the Lord will save me.
Evening and morning and at noon, I will
complain and murmur,
And He will hear my voice.
He will redeem my soul in peace from the battle
which is against me,
For they are many who strive with me.
God will hear and answer them —
Even the one who sits enthroned from of old — Selah.
With whom there is no change,
And who do not fear God.
He has put forth his hands against those who
were at peace with him;
He has violated his covenant.
His speech was smoother than butter,
But his heart was war;
His words were softer than oil,
Yet they were drawn swords.

Cast your burden upon the Lord, and He will sustain you;
He will never allow the righteous to be shaken.
But Thou, O God, wilt bring them down to
the pit of destruction;
Men of bloodshed and deceit will not live out half their days.
But I will trust in Thee.

Psalm 55

6
When You Want to Run Away

Yeats Brown, who thrilled many readers with his book *The Lives of a Bengal Lancer,* used to tell the true story of Yakbu Khan and the sniper. Years ago, while trying to reopen the roads in the Khyber Pass, a connecting route between Pakistan and Afghanistan, the British employees were constantly harassed by a lone sniper who kept picking off workers and soldiers — leaving two or three men dead each day. After three months of this, with their troops fruitlessly searching for the sharpshooter, the British offered a large reward for anyone who could bring in the sniper, dead or alive.

A boy named Yakbu Khan volunteered for the task. The veteran soldiers and workers smiled at the idea of a kid with fuzzy cheeks fulfilling such a difficult mission, but, because he had asked only for a day off and the use of a rifle, they granted his request. Later that day came the crack of a single rifle shot, and news reached the camp that the sniper had been killed. As the boy confidently returned to the valley to collect his reward, the soldiers gathered around to ask him how he had found the sniper, when the crack sharpshooters of the British army had failed to do so. Looking up for a moment from counting his newly acquired wealth, the young boy said, "It was no trouble. I knew all his little tricks and hiding places. He was my father."[1]

Betrayal . . . rejection . . . alienation. To some degree we have all experienced them. We had what seemed to be a good relationship with someone . . . and then, when we were not expecting it, when not prepared for it, that person took careful aim and deliberately shot us in the back, and we felt the searing pain of betrayal.

It is a sad fact that this kind of experience must mar our lives, but it does. Betrayal turns into the entry ramp of our lives and bears down on us, often relentlessly, often without any warning shots, without any sounds of a backfire or a loose muffler, and parks in our front yard.

A RESTLESS COMPLAINT

That happened to King David generations ago, and his story in Psalm 55 could very well be yours today. It begins with an altogether too familiar cry:

> Give ear to my prayer, O God;
> And do not hide Thyself from my supplication.
> Give heed to me, and answer me;
> I am restless in my complaint
> And am surely distracted (vv. 1-2).

Few psalms are more painful than Psalm 55. If we wonder why the cry we hear in these opening verses occurs so often in the psalms, we need only look at ourselves. As each new day begins, we find ourselves facing life all over again, and listening for the rifle shots of betrayal.

It would be a mistake to look for a cool, logical sequence of thought in Psalm 55. There isn't one, because this psalm is forged out of the crucible of pain, and sometimes pain defies logic. Alexander Maclaren describes what is going on here:

> When the heart is writhing within, and tumultuous feelings are knocking at the door of the lips, the words

(we speak) will be troubled and heaped together, and dominant thoughts (of intense emotion) will repeat themselves in defiance of logical continuity.[2]

That is how this song reads. And David tips us off to that in verse 2 when he uses the word *restless.* The word literally means "to wander or to roam aimlessly." When you link that with the rest of the phrase, then David is saying to us, "I am all over the place in my complaint. If it's not one thing, it's another that gets to me. I can't focus or center on just one specific problem area. Lord, it seems that everything is going wrong!"

That sounds familiar. We've all felt that way, and when we do, we are so easily distracted from the things in our lives that we should normally be able to concentrate on . . . like our jobs, our deadlines, our quotas . . . like making lunches for the kids for school . . . or meeting our budget . . . or completing our homework . . . or just being with friends or juggling our calendars. Normally we can deal with those things but not when the pressure of betrayal is tightening like a vice.

A RESENTFUL ENEMY

David understood. You see, his distraction, his distress, was prompted by certain people in his life.

> Because of the voice of the enemy,
> Because of the pressure of the wicked;
> For they bring down trouble upon me,
> And in anger they bear a grudge against me (v. 3).

Apparently, a hostile group of people had formed a pact against him. They felt that they should be in charge rather than David, and now they came after him. The word translated as *trouble* describes the howl of a pursuing pack of wolves, and they were now angrily in pursuit of David. Why that was happening, we are not sure. All we know is that they were hanging on to a grudge. Buried deep in their hearts was something from the past, something David may have done or said that they didn't like. But rather than forgive it, they held on to it, nurtured it, until it began to consume them with rage.

You may know how that works. You may know the sound of the pursuing pack, because you're part of the pack. Your resentment, your grudge-carrying is the fuel that ignites your anger. David Augsburger tells us that the resentful person concludes:

> I've been harboring this anger at those who wronged me for a long time. It has eaten through my stomach, alienated me from others, turned me bitter toward life, and brought me no satisfying relationships, but I think I'll hold on to the resentments a while longer.[3]

But suppressed resentment never dies; it tends to be held in reserve and nurtured like malignant toadstools in the cellar. Resentment suppressed will never lose its power, and like a spark in a gasoline tank, a bit of momentary friction will set off a devastating explosion.

Stop for a moment and think about this question, "How can you tell if inner resentments are lingering beneath the surface of your life?" Before you become like David's wolf-pack enemies, are there some clues to warn you of the impending trouble you may be about to start? I believe there are. Dr. Norman Wright offers these hints related to your potential resentments. Make some mental notes.

1. You feel like striking back or telling off those in authority.
2. You explode for no apparent or obvious reason.
3. You engage in a power struggle with your spouse and view him or her as your enemy.
4. You compare yourself with other family members. You either feel inferior to or compete with them.
5. You make caustic or spiteful comments toward those you love.

6. You feel unappreciated or left out at work or at home.
7. You experience bodily complaints which could include stomachaches, headaches, backaches and so on.
8. Your outlook on life itself is basically pessimistic or negative.[4]

AN ANGUISHED CRY

Depending on your mental checklist, resentment and grudge-carrying may be about to ignite an explosion in your life. It did with David's enemies, and produced an anguished heart in David.

My heart is in anguish within me,
And the terrors of death have fallen upon me.
Fear and trembling come upon me;
And horror has overwhelmed me (vv. 4-5).

The word *anguish* comes from a Hebrew verb that means "to twist or to writhe in pain." It describes violent mental distress to the point that David felt like he could not go on . . . he felt as if he were dying. That's what "the terrors of death" means in verse 4. People who attack you with resentment can do that to you, can't they? David details that heart trouble even further in verse 5. The word *horror* means "to shudder." Under the guns of the enemy, David felt his body out of control with fear. He was shivering from the cold while it was 75 degrees outside. He was wrapped in a blanket watching television, but reaching out to turn up the thermostat. He was drinking a cup of coffee and spilling it on the carpet, because his hand kept shaking. That's what we're talking about here. And my friends, it is not inconsistent with Christianity to be overcome with fear in times of danger and personal attack. And no one knows exactly how he or she will behave in such a situation. So don't judge David harshly.

Some time ago, one man, forty-five, in San Francisco was

diagnosed as having a rare condition. When we have a cut, it heals. When this man cuts his hand, it may take several months before it heals, and his scar tissue only has one-third of the strength that yours and mine have. The cut is very likely to crack open and start bleeding again a year later. But when this man had a severe cut to his head, they actually had to put a steel clamp on his head and leave it there for months.

So it was for David and for some of you. . . . Wounds that take so long to heal . . . wounds that break open and bleed forever . . . when the weapon of assault is bitterness, and resentment.

AN ACT OF BETRAYAL

But, believe it or not, there is one element that makes this even worse. There is one part of the equation that multiplies the damage and that is when a friend, specifically, your closest friend, is the one firing the rifle. Verses 9-11 seem to indicate that the city of Jerusalem had somehow betrayed David. It had been the breeding ground for his enemies and for one in particular. Verses 12 through 14, and 21 and 22 tell of that one:

> For it is not an enemy who reproaches me,
> Then I could bear it;
> Nor is it one who hates me who has exalted himself
> against me,
> Then I could hide myself from him.

> But it is you, a man my equal,
> My companion and my familiar friend.
> We who had sweet fellowship together,
> Walked in the house of God in the throng.

> He has put forth his hand against those
> who were at peace with him;

He has violated his covenant.
His speech was smoother than butter,
But his heart was war;
His words were softer than oil
Yet they were drawn swords.

David was overwhelmed with a sense of abandonment about this atrocious hypocrisy and treachery. He didn't offer any names, but he opened the shutters on his pain. He told us how he was fooled, how his friend broke a covenant with him. There was some kind of legally binding agreement that he wangled his way out of as he stabbed David in the back. He said one thing, and all the time was plotting something different. He'd butter David up, tell him what he needed and perhaps wanted to hear, and then behind his back, rip him to shreds. That hurts, and especially when it's one of your best friends who does the backstabbing.

David and this friend were inseparable. They viewed each other as peers . . . even though David was the king. They talked together about anything and everything. They even went to church together. Their families probably spent a lot of time with each other . . . go-karting . . . fishing . . . sailing . . . skiing . . . You name it, they did it together. And that is a wonderful place to be in your life. To find a godly and wise friend, with whom you can talk about anything without fear, a friend you can turn to when you need advice, encouragement, and support. That is a rare gift. But, sometimes, like David, you get fooled. Somebody slips into your inner circle with less than pure motives, carves out a niche in your life, but then turns the knife on you . . . and the pain is almost unbearable. When those we depend on for love and support betray that trust, we are outraged. Betrayal is a stab in the heart.

I remember sitting in a restaurant about to order lunch. A leader in the church that I pastored had invited me. He wanted to be my friend and adviser. Early on in the conversation he pointed his finger at me and said, "You are not getting to know the *right* people in this church — you need

to meet more monied people . . . people with influence."
My response was to remind him of the prejudicial arro-
gance of his statement. At that moment in time, this
"friend" escalated his campaign against me, and involved
his buddies in the plan. Sometime later one of them visited
my office and told me to "never underestimate their power"
to do what they wanted in that church against me. Both of
these guys fooled me completely and I paid the price.
That's why when Dr. Lewis Smedes adds this observation,
I listen.

> The toughest pain to heal in a committed relationship
> is the pain of betrayal — the wound of a broken trust.
> When trust is broken, we choke on our own commit-
> ment. Betrayal builds a wall between us, around which
> we cannot maneuver. It digs a (gully) between us that
> we cannot bridge. It prevents us from keeping our
> commitment, because it separates us from the person
> who hurt us. And in our hearts we know why. When a
> friend tells our secrets to someone who could hurt us
> with them, she betrays us. When someone we trust
> brutalizes us, with his words or with his hands, he
> betrays us. When a partner demeans us and makes us
> feel less than any human being should feel, she be-
> trays us. When a child we trust steals from us, lies to
> us, becomes our enemy, he betrays us. These are the
> offenses that break our trust. . . . Something lying close
> to our souls cannot indulge treason, not even trivial
> treason. We feel fouled and we feel diminished. Every
> human relationship built on trust is fractured by be-
> trayal. We know it so because we feel the stab so
> deeply.[5]

David's experience is a great teacher for us today. Out of
his pain, his experience of betrayal, we learn some difficult
truths of application.

● It is not unusual for godly people to discover that the
one they thought to be their best friend has become their
greatest enemy.

• The worst thing that a professed enemy can do to us is more tolerable than the treachery and betrayal of a close friend.

OUR NATURAL RESPONSES

When such things happen to us, we naturally respond to them, and usually in one of two ways. Our first response is echoed by David in verses 6 through 8:

> And I said, "Oh that I had wings like a dove!
> I would fly away and be at rest.
> Behold, I would wander far away,
> I would lodge in the wilderness. Selah.
> I would hasten to my place of refuge.
> From the stormy wind and tempest.

David's first thought was to run away, to escape. He pictured in his mind, as I have often done, a place where no one could bother him, attack him, hurt him anymore. He was desperately searching for a place of refuge — where the winds of betrayal didn't reach, and the whip of deception did not crack.

> Then from out of all this [pain] . . . begins that immortal strain — ("O that I had wings like a dove,") which answers to the deepest longings of our soul, and has touched responsive chords in all whose lives are not hopelessly outward and superficial — the longing for a rest, a break. It may be [a dishonorable wish], or perhaps lofty and pure; it may mean only cowardice or laziness; but it is deepest in those who stand unflinchingly at their posts and who are crushed down at times.[6]

It should be of some comfort to us to know that there are spiritual giants who have felt that urge. The desire to withdraw is an attempt to gain protection from the hurts of life by moving away from people. A person who does this becomes detached from people to avoid being hurt or disappointed again. Their unspoken motto is, "If I withdraw, no one can hurt me." We all know the value of solitude, of getting off by ourselves for a time of regrouping. And there is nothing wrong with that. But I sense here that David's desire went deeper. Look at verse 6 again, "And I said, 'O that I had wings like a dove! I would fly away and be at rest." The verb *be at rest* literally means "to settle down, to dwell somewhere." It indicates that David was thinking of a permanent escape. He wanted to run away and not come back. And yes, a godly man or woman can be in such pain that escape seems the only solution. But it is not. Dr. Philip Zimbardo, a respected authority in psychology from Stanford University writes:

> I know of no more potent killer than isolation. There is no more destructive influence on physical and mental health than the isolation of you from me and us from them. It has been shown to be a central agent in the (cause) of depression, paranoia, schizophrenia, rape, suicide . . . and a wide variety of disease states.[7]

In the teeth of betrayal, struggling with the searing pain of deception, another way we respond is with an angry desire for revenge. David, only too human, leaped in that direction.

> Confuse, O Lord, divide their tongues,
> For I have seen violence and strife in the city. . . .
>
> Let death come deceitfully upon them;
> Let them go down alive to Sheol,
> For evil is in their dwelling, in their midst (vv. 9, 15).

In verse 9 David asked God to bring upon his enemies such confusion of counsel, such disruption in their thought patterns, that it would make them powerless to do more evil. But in verse 15, he went further as in a fire of anger, he called down judgment on those who had hurt him so. In fact, if he had the power, he would quite simply get rid of them all by sending them all to hell.

Have you ever wished that on someone? You've been hurt

by people, or life has been unfair to you; therefore, you have the right to strike back. That's what you've told yourself, isn't it? You might even see yourself in these words:

> Have you never tasted the luxury of indulging in hard thoughts against those who have, as you think, injured you? Have you never known what a positive fascination it is to brood over their unkindness, and to pry into their malice, and to imagine all sorts of wrong and uncomfortable things about them? It has made you wretched of course, but it has been a fascinating sort of wretchedness that you could not easily give up.[8]

Do you see what's happening here? The very thing that drove David's enemies toward him—bitterness and grudge-carrying—that same thing is nipping closely at his own heels. It does to all of us. We're a lot like the small boy who was smarting after being punished by his father. Shortly afterward, he knelt by his bed to say his prayers which ended with the usual blessings for the family—all but one. Then he turned to his father who was kneeling beside him and said, "I suppose you noticed you weren't in it."

Abe Lemmons, one-time basketball coach for the University of Texas Longhorns, was asked if he was bitter at Texas Athletic Director, Deloss Dodds, who had fired him. Abe Lemmon replied, "Not at all, but I plan to buy a glass-bottomed car so I can watch the look on his face when I run over him."[9]

A CRY TO THE LORD

We understand that tension. The difference between David and his enemies is not that he didn't feel anger or bitterness in the hurts of life. The difference is what he did with that emotion. His enemies turned it into pain for the others. David turned it into a far better response.

• Look at the first aspect of that response. David called and complained to his God:

As for me, I shall call upon God,
And the Lord will save me.
Evening and morning and at noon,
I will complain and murmur,
And He will hear my voice.
He will redeem my soul in peace
from the battle which is against me (vv. 16-18).

This section of the song returns to a gentler tone. In the extremity of his life, an old habit came back as David turned to God. This entire section is an expression once again of confidence in the Lord's help . . . and in that David found relief and a measure of peace.

But I want you to notice something about David's prayer. Certainly, as the first part of verse 17 indicates, his prayer was consistent and continuous . . . but, more insightful than that, his prayer was also very energetic, very honest and emotional. In verse 17, he said, "I will complain and murmur." The verb translated as *murmur* or *cry aloud* literally means "to growl, to roar, to be boisterous." In other words, David bellowed and still God listened.

It's funny what we think about when it comes to prayer . . . a certain posture — kneeling, eyes closed, correct words and phrases — preferably quiet and reverent. And of course, our prayer should be always positive and thankful. And there is nothing wrong with that. But here, David broke all the rules. For the life of me, I can't see him on his knees, hands folded, eyes closed, quietly speaking to God in worn-out phrases. He was probably on his feet, eyes bulging wide open, veins on his neck popping, fists clenched and shouting. But he was still praying and God was listening.

Bitterness will destroy you internally or it will destroy others externally, unless you begin to deal with it. And one of the ways you do that is to lay it before the Lord in all of its ugliness and awfulness. Give it to Him.

   ● The first response leads naturally to the second response:

Cast your burden upon the Lord,
and He will sustain you;

> He will never allow the righteous to be shaken.
> But Thou, O God, wilt bring them down
> to the pit of destruction; Men of bloodshed and deceit
> will not live out half their days.
> But I will trust in Thee (vv. 22-23).

If you have a study Bible, you'll notice that in the margin the word *burden* is rendered as "what He (God) has given you." And that's its literal sense. Whatever circumstance you find yourself in, whatever pressure or burden weighs you down, at some point you must come to understand that it has been given to you by God. It hasn't taken Him by surprise. He is not standing in heaven, biting His divine fingernails off to the quick trying to solve your problem. He is quite aware of it — it is His gift to you.

In these verses, we are being reminded that we are to tell God all about the problems, the tensions, the pain, and the betrayals of life, but at the same time recognizing and trusting His sovereign gifts to our lives — including the gifts of pain and betrayal. And as that occurs, verse 22 becomes an incredible source of encouragement. The promise is not that God will carry our burden, but rather, that He will support us with it. The promise is not that He will take away the pressure, but that He will hold us up under it. Isn't that great?

And more than that, "He will never allow the righteous to be shaken." Translators have rendered this sentence, "He will not allow His just ones to be continually stressed." "He will not allow the righteous to stagger." "He will not allow the righteous to be harassed forever." God has an amazing ability to step in to our pressures at just the right moment. Years ago, Peter Marshall said:

> It is in times of calamity . . . in days and nights of sorrow and trouble that the presence, the sufficiency and the sympathy of God grow very sure and very wonderful. Then we find out that the grace of God is sufficient for all our needs, for every problem, for

every difficulty, for every broken heart and for every human sorrow.[10]

That was David's conclusion too. What counted for him is that God had the whole thing under control, and that David had chosen to trust Him.

In a dark moment of his life, Hudson Taylor, the great missionary statesman, wrote, "It doesn't matter how great the pressure is. *What really matters is where the pressure lies* — whether it comes between you and God, or whether it presses you nearer His heart."

It did for David . . . who ultimately became known as "the man after God's own heart" — even when the rifle shots of life broke his heart.

Save me, O God,
For the waters have come up to my soul.
I have sunk in deep mire, and there is no foothold;
I have come into deep waters, and a flood overflows me.
I am weary with my crying; my throat is parched;
My eyes fail while I wait for my God.
Those who hate me without a cause are more than
the hairs of my head;
Those who would destroy me are powerful,
What I did not steal, I then have to restore.

O God, it is Thou who dost know my folly,
And my wrongs are not hidden from Thee.
May those who wait for Thee not be ashamed through me,
O Lord God of hosts;
May those who seek Thee not be dishonored through me,
O God of Israel,
Because for Thy sake I have borne reproach;
Dishonor has covered my face.
I have become estranged from my brothers,
And an alien to my mother's sons.

For zeal for Thy house has consumed me,
And the reproaches of those who reproach Thee
have fallen on me.
When I wept in my soul with fasting,
It became my reproach.
When I made sackcloth my clothing,
I became a byword to them.
Those who sit in the gate talk about me,
And I am the song of the drunkards.

But as for me, my prayer is to Thee, O Lord, at
an acceptable time;
O God, in the greatness of Thy lovingkindness,
Answer me with Thy saving truth.
Deliver me from the mire, and do not let me sink;
May I be delivered from my foes, and from the deep waters.
May the flood of water not overflow me,
And may the deep not swallow me up,
And may the pit not shut its mouth on me.

Answer me, O Lord, for Thy lovingkindness is good;
According to the greatness of Thy compassion, turn to me,
And do not hide Thy face from Thy servant,
For I am in distress; answer me quickly.
Oh draw near to my soul and redeem it;
Ransom me because of my enemies!
Thou dost know my reproach and my shame and my dishonor;
All my adversaries are before Thee.

Reproach has broken my heart, and I am so sick.
And I looked for sympathy, but there was none,
And for comforters, but I found none.
And for my thirst they gave me vinegar to drink.

May their table before them become a snare;
And when they are in peace, may it become a trap.
May their eyes grow dim so that they cannot see,
And make their loins shake continually.
Pour out Thine indignation on them,
And may Thy burning anger overtake them.
May their camp be desolate;
May none dwell in their tents.
For they have persecuted him whom Thou Thyself hast smitten,
And they tell of the pain of those whom Thou hast wounded.
Do Thou add iniquity to their iniquity,
And may they not come into Thy righteousness.
May they be blotted out of the book of life,
And may they not be recorded with the righteous.
But I am afflicted and in pain;
May Thy salvation, O God, set me securely on high.
I will praise the name of God with song.
And shall magnify Him with thanksgiving.
And it will please the Lord better than an ox
Or a young bull with horns and hoofs.
The humble have seen it and are glad;
You who seek God, let your heart revive.
For the Lord hears the needy,
And does not despise His who are prisoners.

Let heaven and earth praise Him,
The seas and everything that moves in them.
For God will save Zion and build the cities of Judah,
That they may dwell there and possess it.
And the descendants of His servants will inherit it,
And those who love His name will dwell in it.

Psalm 69

7

When You Can't Stop Crying

In his book *Six Hours One Friday,* Max Lucado writes of an experience that you will understand, like a page from your life. You've walked it . . . you've lived it . . . and you've tried to deal with it.

I had driven by the place countless times. Daily I passed the small plot of land on the way to my office. Daily I told myself, "Someday I need to stop there."

Today, that someday came. I convinced a tightfisted schedule to give me another thirty minutes and I drove in. The intersection appears no different from any other in San Antonio: a Burger King, a Rodeway Inn, a restaurant. But turn northwest, go under the cast-iron sign, and you will find yourself on an island of history that is holding its own against the river of progress. The name on the sign? Locke Hill Cemetery.

As I parked, a darkened sky threatened rain. A lonely path invited me to walk through the 200 + tombstones. The fatherly oak trees arched above me, providing a ceiling for the solemn chambers. Tall grass, still wet from the morning dew, brushed my ankles.

The tombstones, though weathered and chipped, were alive with yesterday. . . . Ruth Lacey is buried there. Born in the days of Napoleon — 1807. Died over a century ago — 1877. I stood on the same spot where a mother wept on a cold day some eight decades past. The tombstone read simply, "Baby Boldty—born and died December 10, 1910." Eighteen-year-old Harry Ferguson was laid to rest in 1883 under these words, "Sleep sweetly, tired young pilgrim." I wondered what *wearied* him so.

Then I saw it. It was chiseled into a tombstone on the northern end of the cemetery. The stone marks the destination of the body of Grace Llewellen Smith. No date of birth is listed, no date of death. Just the names of her two husbands, and this epitaph:

Sleeps, but rests not.
Loved, but was loved not.
Tried to please, but pleased not.
Died as she lived—alone.

Words of futility. I stared at the marker and wondered about Grace Llewellen Smith. I wondered about her life. I wondered if she'd written the words . . . or just lived them. I wondered if she deserved the pain. I wondered if she was bitter or beaten. I wondered if she was plain. I wondered if she was beautiful. I wondered why some lives are so fruitful while others are so futile. I caught myself wondering aloud, "Mrs. Smith, what broke your heart?"

Raindrops smudged my ink as I copied the words: "Loved, but was loved not . . . "

Long nights. Empty beds. Silence. No response to messages left. No return to letters written. No love exchanged for love given.

"Tried to please, but pleased not . . . "

I could hear the hatchet of disappointment.

"How many times do I have to tell you?" Chop.

"You'll never amount to anything." Chop. Chop.

"Why can't you do anything right?" Chop, chop, chop.

"Died as she lived—alone."

How many Grace Llewellen Smiths are there? How many people will die in the loneliness in which they are living? The homeless in Atlanta. The happy-hour hopper in Los Angeles. The bag lady in Miami. The preacher in Nashville. Any person who doubts whether the world needs him. Any person who is convinced that no one really cares. Any person who had been given a ring, but never a heart; criticism, but never a chance; a bed, but never rest. These are the victims of futility. And unless someone intervenes, unless something happens, the epitaph of Grace Smith will be theirs.[1]

AN AWFUL ALONENESS

Psalm 69, although etched across the life of David some 3,000 years ago, could just as easily have been found inscribed on the tombstone of Grace Llewellen Smith in San Antonio in 1988, because it too was written by a person in crisis. This psalm reveals a vulnerable man who could not shrug off slander, betrayal, loneliness, or persecution. Psalm 69 is an individual's lament. It was written by David, but it could have been written by Grace, or Tom, or Kathy, or Bob, or Carol . . . or you!

Save me, O God,
For the waters have come up to my soul.

I have sunk in deep mire, and there is no foothold;
I have come into deep waters, and a flood overflows me. I am weary with my crying; my throat is parched;
My eyes fail while I wait for my God (vv. 1-3).

These verses speak of inner turmoil and floundering. The word *waters* pictures overwhelming distress and danger. What we have described here is the fearful anxiety of a man who is no longer able to see beyond his adversity, who is afraid of being swallowed up or having the ground pulled out from under him. Joseph Parker, a wonderful nineteenth-century preacher describes the scene vividly:

The man can do nothing. Here is an image of helplessness, of dire despair. So long as a man can run or walk

or defend himself in any degree, his dejection is saved
from despair; but the process of sinking—that is a
doctor's word. The doctor says, "The patient is sinking,
slipping." We know the meaning of the expression;
there is no longer any sphere of combat or defense;
the motion is (only) downward.[2]

So true was that for David that he said he was worn out
from crying. He had cried so long and so hard there was
nothing left. Oh, like a typical male, he probably didn't cry
in front of anybody, but maybe in his car on the interstate it
was different. . . . maybe at the office, with the door locked,
he let it out.

Maybe, some Monday night, downstairs when he was
supposed to be watching Monday night football . . . maybe
there, all alone . . . he wept until he was too weary to even
watch the rest of the game.

Weariness is tough. I don't mean the physical weariness
that comes with mowing the lawn, or the mental weariness
that follows a hard day of decisions and thinking. No . . .
I'm thinking about the emotional weariness that comes just
before you give up, the kind David encountered.

But such weariness usually doesn't exist by itself. Its
shadow, its mirror image, its inseparable twin is an overwhelming sense of loneliness and heartbreak.

> Reproach has broken my heart, and I am so sick.
> And I looked for sympathy but there was none,
> And for comforters, but I found none.
> They also gave me gall for my food,
> And for my thirst they gave me vinegar to drink (vv.
> 20-21).

The word *reproach* refers to sharp things that people said
against David. Other translations of this verse put it this
way, "Insults have broken my heart." "Abuse has broken
my spirit and I am ill, depressed." David's enemies had
broken through his weary defenses and caught him with his
guard down. They kept coming and coming until he finally

crumbled. And when he thought that perhaps they would go away, they "gave him gall for food, and vinegar to drink," meaning they kept hammering him with a cruel and nonstop attack.

David would have understood comedian Jonathan Winters who, referring to his parents' divorce forty years earlier, said, "All of my humor is a response to sorrow."[3] I identify with that. The day my own parents divorced was and *is* a day of excruciating sorrow . . . a sorrow that will never completely leave. Oh, I love my parents, see them regularly, and they each come and visit our family — separately of course. We have good relationships. Even as I write this paragraph, I am at my mother's vacation spot — a lovely trailer in Canada. I love them both dearly, but I understand David's sorrow.

In the midst of it, he looked around for some support, some comfort of any kind. He looked for a firm handshake, for an arm around the shoulder, or a hug; he waited all evening for the phone to ring; or for somebody to drop by and talk, but it never happened. No comforters arrived, no messages were left on his answering machine, no cards came in the mail.

Our English word *comfort* translates from the Latin *cum fortis* and means "to give strength." That's what he needed! Think about that. Here is a very visible and popular king, surrounded by people, yet all alone. You see, loneliness has little to do with being all by yourself. You can be in a crowd and still be lonely. Loneliness is that pain or emptiness you feel when you are socially or emotionally isolated from close relationships. It's the feeling of nothing to do and no one to do it with.

All of us know about the chilling effects of loneliness. It's a cold, gray mist that filters in and around our hearts. You try turning up the heat or dressing warmer, but it isn't very effective in warding off the chill. It's a cold that seems to settle in the very marrow of our bones. . . . [4]

EMOTIONAL STRESS

The foglike mist that surrounds you becomes more dense
when pressure and pain thicken the fog.

> And do not hide Thy face from Thy servant,
> For I am in distress; answer me quickly.
>
> But I am afflicted and in pain;
> May Thy salvation, O God, set me securely on high
> (vv. 17, 29).

The words *distress* and *affliction* refer to pressure, to stress
that brings with it mental pain. I think we can understand
that. I know I can. I ended up in the hospital, running for a
stress test, being photographed as part of an echocardium
to be sure my heart was okay, and found out that it was.
But the real culprit was stress and pressure. I stand alongside David.

> In the past thirty years, doctors and health officials
> have come to realize how heavy a toll stress is taking
> on the nation's well-being. According to the American
> Academy of Family Physicians, two-thirds of office vis-
> its to family doctors are prompted by stress-related
> symptoms. At the same time, leaders of industry have
> become alarmed by the huge cost of such symptoms in
> absenteeism, company medical expenses and lost pro-
> ductivity.[5]

Every day we Americans consume twenty-eight tons of
aspirins, tranquilizers and sleeping pills. All of us experience some of that stress.[6] And because of that, David's
experience is not so remote, and his tears don't seem so
embarrassing, after all. And that is especially true when you
consider specifically what was prompting all of this. David
talks about it throughout this psalm. There are at least three
reasons for his tears.

The first reason is found back in verse 4—David was a
hated man. Notice how he remembers it:

Those who hate me without a cause
are more than the hairs of my head;
Those who would destroy me are powerful,
What I did not steal, I then have to restore.

We don't know much about the circumstances surrounding this psalm. But what we do know is that David's enemies were making false accusations against him, fueled by their hatred.

And David was confused because he was being treated as guilty, although he was innocent. Now he may be overstating the situation. When you're under the gun that often happens   *everybody* is against you, plotting, antagonizing. Maybe there is some exaggeration here, but being hated is a heart-wrenching experience, especially when you haven't done anything!

Have you ever had someone hate you? I mean really hate you? It wasn't your imagination, it wasn't paranoia, or exaggeration. It wasn't simply dislike or annoyance — it was bone-chilling hate.

That's tough to deal with. You keep asking yourself, "Why is this happening to me?" I read a great answer to that question recently from David Dickson, a Scottish pastor in the early seventeenth century.

Holiness and integrity will not necessarily ward off the (hostility) of a wicked world. It is not strange to see truly godly people at odds with people who are in power and authority in society. He that is most godly may be troubled and hated without reason, and may be treated as a thief, even though honest.[7]

Believe it or not, it is often the most spiritually healthy and advanced among us who are called on to suffer in the most agonizing ways. And one of those ways is to be hated. The unfortunate part would be if you are doing the hating, inflicting the pain. That should not be. Alex Haley, author of the book *Roots,* wrote about this, "Hate at its best will destroy you; but it will always immobilize you."[8]

ESTRANGEMENT

Hate like that has no place in the church any more than it did in David's experience. But there it was and it produced tears. As did the dishonor and separation he endured from his family and friends. Look at verses 7 and 8:

> Because for Thy sake I have borne reproach;
> Dishonor has covered my face.
> I have become estranged from my brothers,
> And an alien to my mother's sons.

David talks about being *dishonored.* The word means "to be disgraced or insulted." What was happening? David was walking through a mine-field experience that has repeated itself without number since his time. His friends, and family, although they probably stood beside him initially, ultimately bailed out on him. As time wore on, and the accusations and hatred did not stop, they started to believe the reports.

The word *estranged* in verse 8 means "to turn aside from someone." When his pain was the greatest, his own family turned away from him and he became "an alien" to his own brothers. *Alien* means "unknown, unfamiliar." In other words, in turning their backs on David, they lost touch. They didn't see his children grow up; they didn't spend holidays together. There were family reunions, but David wasn't invited.

At its worst extreme, being ignored makes people feel insignificant. At the deepest psychological level, they can feel as if they don't exist. That's where David stood, as you may also. An eighty-four-year-old woman, living in a run-down apartment in Los Angeles sent this message to the *Los Angeles Times:* "I'm so lonely I could die — so alone. I cannot write. My fingers and hands pain me. I see no human beings. My phone never rings. . . . I never hear from no one . . . never have any kind of holidays, no kind. My birthday is this month. . . . Isn't anyone else lonely like me? . . . I don't know what to do." She enclosed some stamps and a one-dollar bill hoping that someone would either call or write her. When a newsman called her, she burst into tears.[9]

David wept because he was dishonored and separated from the people he loved. But not only was he hated; it went further than that. . . . he endured again intense verbal persecution. Maybe you've wondered, as I have, why so many times throughout the ancient Hebrew hymnal, the lashing of peoples' tongues is so prevalent. I suppose there is really no mystery to it. Of all our pain, it is this that is most prevalent and most tolerated within the church and our lives. So it was with David.

For zeal for Thy house has consumed me.
And the reproaches of those who reproach Thee
have fallen on me.

Zeal means "ardor or jealousy" in the spirit that longs to see cleansing and revival. That had gripped David's life. And yet, because he was gripped by God's cause, he became the object of assault.

When I wept in my soul with fasting,
It became my reproach.
When I made sackcloth my clothing,
I became a byword to them (vv. 10-11).

David's signs of humility and repentance (fasting and sackcloth), made him a laughingstock, rather than bringing his people to repentance. Matters had even gone so far that even in the gate of the city—the place where business and law were conducted—he was a joke.

Those who sit in the gate talk about me,
And I am the song of the drunkards (v. 12).

David's earnestness of faith and his concern for God's honor made him an object of dislike, a target of drunken ridicule. I wonder how many Christians have been brought to tears because we have stood for righteousness. I wonder how many of us have known persecution because of our identification with Jesus Christ. If our lives are characterized by ease, if there have been no problems because of our faith, there is every likelihood that something is wrong.

In the country of Nepal they understand what David was going through. In 1980 there were approximately 500 Christians in that country. The penalty for becoming a Christian was one year in prison, and two years for leading someone to Christ. And yet, in seven years, 95,000 people have come to know Christ and there are over 67,000 believers meeting weekly in home Bible studies. You see, the Christians were leading so many of the prison personnel to Christ that the authorities reacted by removing the Christians from prison.

If we Christians were to compromise less, we would undoubtedly suffer more. *Faithfulness* to Jesus Christ will bring ridicule and alienation and this should not surprise us, for we are followers of the suffering Christ.

Now that doesn't mean that it won't bother us. It doesn't mean that we won't be incredibly hurt. And it doesn't mean that we won't cry. When we are hated without cause; when our own family and friends dishonor and alienate us, when we are forced to endure persecution because of our faith, it takes its toll.

But the faith that honors God is the faith that has come up through all the betrayals and inequities of life. . . . and stands above them. We do not want some secretly gained faith that has never been tested by the weather. We want a faith that has encountered the enemy all the way, that has come to the top by the grace and goodness of God. Be very wary of people who have never gone through difficult circumstances, who have never encountered the enemy, who have never seen the wilderness of pain. But have confidence in the people who have seen it all—disloyalty, unbelief, deception, hatred, and slander, and yet have left them behind. Those are the people who make their impress on the world.

RESPONSE TO SUFFERING

Such people, like David, know how to respond to the tears of life. Briefly follow David's path of response.

● First of all, he turned to God, through his tears, with a prayer for *compassion.*

> But as for me, my prayer is to Thee, O Lord,
> at an acceptable time;
> O God, in the greatness of Thy loving-kindness,
> Answer me with Thy saving truth. . . .
>
> Answer me, O Lord, for Thy lovingkindness is good;
> According to the greatness of Thy compassion,
> turn to me (vv. 13, 16).

These verses concentrate on the Lord's goodness and mercy. David asked for relief based on the compassion of God. But notice, he submitted to God's time. The word *acceptable* in verse 13 means "that which pleases God." David, in the midst of his tears, humbly admitted that however urgent his need was for a quick answer, still, his time was in God's hand.

There is a mystery here. We are the instant generation — we want God to be as fast as McDonald's. Often, however, He isn't. But David, even in his pain, did not presume upon God. He knew that in His time of grace, the answer would come. That's the first part of our heart's response.

● The second response is one we will all identify with. David, out of his crucible of pain, begged God to exact His judgment on those who pursued him.

> May their table before them become a snare;
> And when they are in peace, may it become a trap.
> May their eyes grow dim so that they cannot see,
> And make their loins shake continually.
> Pour out Thine indignation on them,
> And may Thy burning anger overtake them.
> May their camp be desolate;

May none dwell in their tents.
For they have persecuted him
whom Thou Thyself hast smitten,
And they tell of the pain of those
whom Thou hast wounded.
Do Thou add iniquity to their iniquity,
And may they not come into Thy righteousness.
May they be blotted out of the book of life,
And may they not be recorded with the righteous
(vv. 22-28).

David didn't miss much as he called for God to act. Upon first reading it appears mean and hot-tempered — vindictive even. But we must remember that David was in an extreme crisis. Also, he experienced the attack upon himself as an attack upon God. In calling for God's judgment, he was calling for the vindication of God's name.

Please don't miss the fact that David did not exact the judgment himself. Instead, he turned it over to God. That's hard to do. When you're taking it in the neck, your first inclination is to strike back, to inflict pain for pain, suffering for suffering. That is a natural instinct of the heart, but David fought it off. He appealed to God for mercy. . . . and left the action to God. You may need to do that. Maybe you're facing an extreme situation of pain at home. . . . your marriage partner has misused you. . . . hurt you. You might even need to leave for your own protection; but don't plot revenge. If you're divorced, give up the paybacks. Some people you trusted have abused that trust. They've slandered you, and created pain and tears in your life.

● Leave them to God, and move on. David did. Look at his third response.

I will praise the name of God with song,
And shall magnify Him with thanksgiving.
And it will please the Lord better than an ox
Or a young bull with horns and hoofs.
The humble have seen it and are glad;
You who seek God, let your heart revive.

For the Lord hears the needy,
And does not despise His who are prisoners.
Let heaven and earth praise Him.
The seas and everything that moves in them
(vv. 30-34).

In these verses we see a decided shift in the tone of the psalm. Up to this point, crisis has been the heartbeat. Suddenly, the psalmist shifts to a focus on worship, praise and thanksgiving as *hope breaks in.* But his worship and praise and thanksgiving did not come until he had *given up* his personal desire for revenge. Do you see that? Some of you wonder why there is no joy, no thanksgiving in your life. Now you know! Alexander Maclaren reminds us of how essential our praise and thanksgiving is to our well-being when he writes:

The life which is at all influenced by thanksgiving will be pure, strong, (joyful), in its continual counting of its gifts and in its thoughts of the Giver. . . . the noblest offering that we can bring, the only (satisfaction) that Christ asks, is that our hearts and our lives should say, "We thank Thee, O Lord." And the continual thanksgiving will ensure continuous growth in our Christian character, and a constant increase in the strength and depth of our faith.[10]

• Some of us will never go any further in our faith. Because we are riveted to the pain of the past, to the tears, we will not let go of our bitterness, our revenge. Yet, it must happen, if the fourth response of our heart is to occur.

O God, it is Thou who dost know my folly,
And my wrongs are not hidden from Thee.
May those who wait for Thee not be ashamed through me, O Lord God of hosts;
May those who seek Thee not be dishonored through me, O God of Israel (vv. 5-6).

This is an incredible response in the midst of tears. David was innocent, yet he was very conscious that God knew him more deeply than he knew himself. So, he didn't claim to be perfect in his responses to the pain and suffering in his life. But he was very concerned now that his life not be a stumbling block to others. You see, when a believer is suffering, is persecuted for righteous living, the rest of us are waiting to see what happens. David prayed that his own reactions to suffering would not adversely affect the work of God. These verses demonstrate the selfless concern that only a person committed to God can display.

David could have said, "Listen, I'm the one who has been wronged. I'm the one who has been hurt. I'm the one who deserves better." Instead, he pled with God not to let his possible overreactions to his situation harm the people close to him, the ones watching him.

Is that your desire? Make it be.

*But if any of you lacks wisdom, let him ask of God,
who gives to all men generously and without reproach,
and it will be given to him. But let him ask in
faith without any doubting, for the one who doubts
is like the surf of the sea driven and tossed by
the wind. For let not that man expect that he will
receive anything from the Lord, being a double-minded
man, unstable in all his ways.*

*But let the brother of humble circumstances glory in
his high position; and let the rich man glory in
his humiliation, because like flowering grass he
will pass away. For the sun rises with a
scorching wind, and withers the grass; and its
flower falls off, and the beauty of its appearance
is destroyed; so too the rich man in the midst
of his pursuits will fade away.*

*Blessed is a man who perseveres under trial;
for once he has been approved, he will receive
the crown of life, which the Lord has
promised to those who love Him.*

James 1:5-12

8
Wisdom for
Difficult Days

Jim Bishop writes great human interest stories. Several years ago he wrote about a very talented woman named Paula who was the top literary agent in New York. With 180 authors under contract, she had an uncanny sense of talent and timing. Jim Bishop worked with her and described her as "fortyish, given to wearing pleated wool skirts, an elaborate nose, and by any standard ugly."

Jim writes that one day a very crude and earthy cowboy came into the office with a manuscript. Paula properly put him in his place. And so he sat there anxiously as she glanced through his manuscript. "Mr. McGowan?" Paula said, as she raised her eyes from the manuscript. "Red McGowan? This manuscript has possibilities."

And, as per the normal course, they got his particulars. He was thirty-four. He owned a small ranch in the Sierras in California, and he wrote his plots under a kerosene lamp. The cowboy then asked Paula for lunch. "Don't go," Jim Bishop advised. But Paula said yes, and within four days, she and Red McGowan were having both lunch and dinner together. "I love you ... will you marry me?" he blurted out suddenly.

But he made it tough on her. "I've got to go back home and hug my cows," he said ... and so he gave her a long train ticket with very involved directions. He told her, "You catch the train from New York to Chicago and then from Chicago to Los Angeles. There take a day to look at Hollywood, or do whatever you'd like. At midnight, you catch the train and you'll arrive in my little town at 5:40 A.M. Now, if you love me at all, you'll be there at 5:40 A.M., two weeks from today."

Paula had never been a sentimental person, but she cried and kissed everyone good-bye. "I'm going off to the great perhaps," she said over her shoulder, and headed for Chicago, then to Los Angeles, and then to the midnight train to this little town. At 5:40 A.M. the train stopped. She got off and saw nothing but sagebrush. There wasn't a sign of a human being.

"There's no fool like an old fool," she thought to herself. Paula looked at her watch, and wondered when the next train would come by. But suddenly from around the corner came Red McGowan. He scooped her up in his arms . . . kissed her . . . married her . . . loved her.

Two years later he died of cancer, even though there was no sign of it when he had first fallen in love. After burying Red, Paula went back to their home, sat in the kitchen, and turned on the gas.[1]

Unable to face the extremities of her life she concluded that life was not worth living. To some degree we have all leaned in that direction. If we have not contemplated ending life, then most certainly we have thought about running away from difficulties. There are times when it seems that we cannot go on, that we cannot take it anymore and we wonder how we will cope.

James, the half brother of Jesus, wondered aloud about that same question. Fortunately for us, he wrote down his wonderings, grafting into his epistle thoughts about the extremities of our lives and how we respond to them. He wanted us to be able to face our problems wisely, to live our lives as Christians appropriately. He addressed that idea in the first chapter of his book.

Consider it all joy, my brethren,
when you encounter various trials. . . .

But if any of you lacks wisdom, let him ask of God,
who gives to all men generously and without reproach,
and it will be given to him (vv. 2, 5).

The immediate context, you'll remember from chapter 3, is the trials in our lives and our ability to deal with them. Often the pain is so severe, the trauma so unsettling, that we have difficulty accepting them, let alone understanding them. We need insight so that we can go on living and not become bogged down in the quicksand of difficulty.

Verse 5 is God's offer of wisdom. Now wisdom means something much more than knowledge or intellectual ability, for these are often found to be totally inadequate in dealing with life's deepest problems. What is described here is "practical wisdom." It is knowledge turned into action, especially in the difficult circumstances and problems of life. The wise Christian sees life and its problems from God's perspective, and as a result, is able to see those problems as opportunities for growth. And with that perspective he or she will be able to make personal decisions and progress toward maturity. Scott Peck, in his intriguing book *The Road Less Traveled*, explains why this is so necessary.

It is in this whole process of meeting and solving problems that life has its meaning. Problems are the cutting edge that distinguishes between success and failure. Problems call forth. . . . courage and wisdom. It is only because of problems that we grow mentally and spiritually. . . . It is for this reason that wise people learn not to dread but actually to welcome problems. . . .

Most of us are not so wise. Fearing the pain involved, almost all of us . . . attempt to avoid problems. We procrastinate, hoping that they will go away. We ignore them, forget them, pretend they do not exist. . . . We attempt to skirt around problems and the emotional suffering inherent in them is the primary basis of all human mental illness.[2]

But God does not want this to occur in our lives. He offers us wisdom, which is the skill of living life successfully. In the midst of our difficult circumstances, God longs to give us the ability we need to face our problems ... and grow through them. According to these verses, God desires that we progress to maturity. And verse 5 indicates that He will not hold back from us the wisdom we need.

When we don't have wisdom, the problem is not with God but with us. We may set up *roadblocks* to appropriating God's wisdom. Although He desires that we operate in the sphere of wisdom, we may not want what He wants. And James was sharp enough to identify four different kinds of roadblocks to wisdom in our lives.

CONSISTENT DOUBT

But let him ask in faith without any doubting,
for the one who doubts is like the surf of the sea,
driven and tossed by the wind.
For let not that man expect that he will receive
anything from the Lord (vv. 6-7).

When we are battered and bruised by the pressures and difficulties of life, the first questions that ricochet from our hearts are, "Why, Lord, why this ... why now ... why me?" Invariably we come to God with those questions. We come looking for answers, for wisdom to understand.

But James says that God gives Himself only to those who want what He gives. That's the impact of the phrase "to ask in faith." That refers to an essential attitude of the heart, where a person is totally convinced of the power, love, grace, and mercy of God. To pray in faith is to exhibit a wholehearted attitude of unquestioning commitment to God and a dependence on Him.

You see, when we ask God for wisdom, we must believe not only in God's ability to respond to our prayers, but also in His willingness to do so in conformity to His nature and will. One commentator explains it this way:

> There must . . . be a trust (an element implicit in the biblical word *faith*) that God's way is best, whatever it is. Arguing with God, complaining about circumstances, or hesitancy to be open to His answer are human attitudes that will prevent God from responding.[3]

And yet that is where we have the most trouble. Notice how James identifies this trouble in verse 6, "But let him ask in faith without any doubting." The word *doubting* means "to be divided, to be at variance with yourself."

Doubting is our inner uncertainty about whether we really want the answer God has for us. We're often very much like the fellow who was on the roof of his two-story home, fixing his television antenna. Just then a strong gust of wind blew him off balance and he slid down the roof, saving himself by grabbing onto the edge of the gutter.

In the grip of panic and fear he yelled into the sky, "Is there anybody up there who can help me?" To his amazement a voice thundered from the heavens, "I am here. I will help." The man shouted, "What should I do? Please, help me!" To which the voice replied, "Let go of the edge and trust me." After a few moments of silence, the man looked again to the sky and yelled, "Is there anybody else up there who can help me?"

That's how a doubter behaves — he's not sure about God's answers. He is a walking civil war in whom trust and distrust of God wage a continual battle. At one moment he wants what God has, and in the next, he doesn't.

Certainly, questions are normal, but we must not stay there. We are not to second-guess our God, thinking all the time, "He's lost it . . . He doesn't know what He is doing . . . nor does He even care about me."

That's part of what James was driving at when he talked

about doubting. But even more, doubters want help from God, but only when they feel they absolutely need it. When things are going well, they put God on the shelf. But in a crisis, when they are unable to handle the situation, they turn to God. Dr. Doug Moo, who teaches at Trinity Evangelical Divinity School, puts it this way:

> The divided person has no fixed beliefs and direction. He is prey to every.... contrary storm of opposition and persecution, and his loyalty to God is constantly threatened. He does not possess that unwavering confidence in God, uninfluenced by adversity . . . [4]

Brian Sternberg has that kind of confidence. He could have been an Olympic hero. He set a new world record for the pole vault, but within a month after that success he had an accident and was paralyzed from the neck down. While Brian was in the hospital, his uncle came to him and said, "Oh, I wish I could take your place for a week and give you some rest." Brian replied, "You couldn't do it. I know because I couldn't either, if I didn't have to." In an interview for a nationwide magazine, Brian was asked what his faith in God meant to him at this time in his life. He said, "I want to know that my life is being used fully for the glory of God. . . . Having faith is a necessary step toward one of two things. Being healed is one of them. Peace of mind, if healing doesn't come, is the other. Either one will suffice."[5]

INSTABILITY OF LIFE

Look at verse 8, " . . . being a double-minded man, unstable in all his ways." The word *double-minded* is one that James himself may have coined. It literally means "two-souled." It is as though one soul declares, "I believe," and the other shouts, "I don't." It is related to doubt, but goes deeper. It produces instability, an unsettled attitude, an inconsistency of life.

James is saying that if we are not secure with God, then we are not secure at all. He is describing a person who cannot maintain a steady course or direction in life. We must realize that when a person has no stable understanding of God and, therefore, no firm relationship with Him, he can have no truly satisfying philosophy of life. If one does not know that God is sovereign and controls all things, then adversity can be incredibly frightening. In fact, a sense of hopelessness, despair, panic, or depression is often the result. Such a person invariably tends to see himself as a victim of circumstances, rather than a participant in the life and program of God.

One of the frightening features of the present day is the widespread dependence on sedatives and other pseudo solutions to cope with situations which our grandparents would not have seen as problems — ordinary tasks like bringing up children, facing a tomorrow which is essentially the same as today, boredom, and restlessness.

The cynic would say that the problem today is not, "Is there life after death?" but, "Is there life before death?" People find themselves no longer able to face the grind of making ends meet; or they are dealt savage blows through disease or circumstance, and they have no resource by which to make their way effectively through such hazards. But in their instability, they forget to look to God. Richard Halverson, Chaplain to the U.S. Senate, speaks precisely to that point:

Either God is. Or God is not. If God is not, nothing else matters anyway. Humanity will go on doing the best it can with scientific and technological progress, perennially victimized by our own selfishness, failure, and sin, refining the instruments of our own destruction.

And if God is . . . then either He is in charge of history, or He is not.

If He is not, mankind is without hope. His aspirations are illusions. Life is irrational and absurd.

But the Bible records the exciting fact that God is in charge! He is the Author of History. He is the Lord of History. There is hope—even for sinful, hedonistic, selfish mankind. God loves, He cares, and nothing is impossible for Him!

As someone has said, history is His story. Jesus Christ was very clear on this: History is linear; history is going somewhere; it has a beginning and an end, and a process in between. Eternity is endless—but not static. Eternity is dynamic.

History has purpose. Life has meaning. Life has destiny.[6]

But a double-souled person doesn't see that, and as a result mires himself in instability. But sometimes even we who are believers are guilty of this same instability. When James refers to instability, he not only is referring to one's relationship with God, but also to personal character, to an inner division and insecurity which shows up in all of our experiences, good or bad. For a believer whose commitment to God is thin at the best of times, that kind of instability will mark his life. In his personal life, his business life, his social life, as well as his spiritual life, there will be an indecisiveness. Inconsistency in his faith will characterize him.

How unfortunate that is. But it is not surprising, because a person who doesn't trust anyone, including God at times, cannot hope to be anything but up and down in life. A.W. Tozer speaks to this:

What we need very badly these days is a company of Christians who are prepared to trust God as completely now as they know they must do at the last day. For each of us the time is surely coming when we shall have nothing but God. Health and wealth and friends and hiding places will all be swept away and we shall have only God. To the man of pseudo faith that is a terrifying thought, but to real faith it is one of the most comforting thoughts that the heart can entertain.[7]

SELF-DEPRECIATION

Look at verse 9, "But let the brother of humble circumstances glory in his high position." The words *humble circumstances* literally mean "without possessions, insignificant." It should not surprise us that the great majority of people who have followed Jesus Christ have been poor. When these people became Christians, they discovered rather quickly that following Christ did not automatically solve their economic problems. If you find yourself in that situation, it is easy to view yourself as unimportant and insignificant. In fact, when it comes to difficulties in your life, you might find yourself thinking, "I'm too poor for God to be interested in me. I'm a no-name Christian. I'm not important to anyone. . . . least of all God. Why would He be interested in my problems?"

James knew that many to whom he wrote were living in grinding poverty and needed encouragement to know that God cared for them too. That's why he told them to glory in their high position. The verb *glory* is sometimes translated as "rejoice." This person who feels so insignificant is told to rejoice "in his high position," which is a reference to his spiritual position in Christ. One commentator suggests:

> The one, against whom lifes' tides seem to be running, and who is lowly as the world sees things, needs to seek to live in a sustained awareness of the heights to which he has been lifted in Christ.[8]

By forgiving us, and giving us eternal life through Jesus Christ, God lifts us up and gives us new dignity and worth. And James is telling us that even if we find ourselves on the low end of the world's rating system, in God's eyes we matter. Someone has said, "Call no man worthless for whom Christ died." That is so good. A believer can hold his head high because of his spiritual position.

James is teaching us that we should view our situation, however insignificant it may appear to be, not through the cloudy lens of our society but through the clear telescope of God's perspective. We live in a world which believes that happiness consists in the amount of stuff we own. If we have the right house, the right car, the right professions, then we will be truly alive. That is so wrong. Even though these first-century believers had lost virtually everything, they could still rejoice because they were spiritually wealthy . . . and embraced by the love of God.

SELF-SUFFICIENCY

This final roadblock to wisdom is the opposite of self-depreciation. Look at verses 10 and 11:

> And let the rich man glory in his humiliation,
> because like flowering grass he will pass away.
> For the sun rises with a scorching wind,
> and withers the grass; and its flower falls off,
> and the beauty of its appearance is destroyed;
> so too the rich man in the midst of his pursuits
> will fade away.

The great peril of riches is that they tend to give a false sense of security. People begin to feel that they are safe, that they have the resources necessary to cope with anything that comes along. Even in the midst of difficulty there can emerge from the cocoon of self-sufficiency an attitude that says, "I don't need God's or anyone's help, and if I run into any snags, I can buy my way out of trouble." That attitude is reflected in the bumper sticker that says, "Them that has the gold makes the rules." People believe that and develop a self-sufficiency rather than a God-dependency. But that philosophy doesn't work. The author of *The Rage Within*, Dr. Willard Gaylin, tells us what it is really like:

> By assuming that material things would buy happiness, we designed our goals in that direction. When the paths seemed to lead to no reward, we assumed

we must traverse them still further. The assumption was wrong, but by the time we discovered that we had been driving ourselves down a path that led nowhere, we were too frightened, too discouraged, too exhausted to look for other roads to pleasure. We had already sacrificed our youth, our pleasure in the company of our children (who are no longer children and no longer surround us), our imagination and our undeveloped resources. We feel deprived at the most fundamental level. We feel robbed of the very meaning of existence. And we will rage at the irretrievable loss.[9]

James reminds us that if God's wisdom is our goal, and we find ourselves in the position of having wealth, we must then adopt a proper perspective on life. The rich man is to "glory in his humiliation." Believers who happen to enjoy material things are to look to the place of sin from which Christ has saved us. To our possessions we must say, "But oh, what a sinner I am!"

James is urging the rich to stop putting their trust in that which their own power assembles. He urges them to admit their essential human helplessness and humbly put their trust in God. James is saying, "Let people know your riches are not the most important thing in your life—not just with words, but with your actions. Let people know that your eternal perspective is far more important than your earthly perspective."

You see, the point is . . . if you don't learn that now . . . you may be forced to learn it when it all disappears. But by then, you may be beyond teaching. The image of these two verses is that unexpectedly, in the midst of a very busy, high charging day—it can all be gone. Worse than that . . . you can have it all . . . and still find that you don't have a lease on life . . . that your wife can die of cancer just like anyone else's . . . that your kid can run away from home, as fast, if not faster than anyone else's . . . that you can suffer a heart attack, regardless of your investment portfolio. That's the lesson. There are many things that no amount of money

can buy. Think of it this way: "Money will buy a bed, but
not sleep. Books, but not brains. Food, but not appetite. A
house, but not a home. Medicine, but not health. Amuse-
ment, but not happiness. Finery, but not beauty. A crucifix,
but not a Savior."[10]

A CROWN OF LIFE

My friends, life hurts sometimes, doesn't it? So how in the
world are we to steer a course to the goal of spiritual maturity? Only by appropriating the wisdom God gives, a wisdom that allows us to see things from His perspective, a
wisdom that makes us see earth in the light of heaven and
eternal life. When that happens, what will be the results in
this life?

> Blessed is a man who perseveres under trial;
> for once he has been approved,
> he will receive the crown of life,
> which the Lord has promised to those
> who love Him (v. 12).

The word *blessed* refers to a distinctive joy, an inner
quality of life, reflected in peace, contentment, and satisfaction that can be sustained in spite of difficulties. How ab-
sent that is from so many people's lives. In her book *The
Plateauing Trap,* Judith Bardwick describes a typical situation from her management files.

> I'm forty-seven and I don't know what to do. My
> whole life is boring. All I ever seem to do is meet my
> responsibilities, and I'm tired of it. Every morning I
> get up and go to work and come home. When I come
> home it's the same old routine. I read the paper, eat
> supper, do some work, watch television, and go to bed.
> Then I get up and I go to work again.
>   I guess my life is pretty much like everybody else's,
> but the truth is, I'm feeling old. I'm too young to feel
> old! There's nothing exciting going on. Work used to

be exciting. That's when I put everything into it. But now I've gone as far as I'm going to go. What am I going to do with the rest of my life? I hate the thought that it's going to be like this forever.[11]

James is telling us who walk in God's wisdom that there is a different quality of life available to us now. That emphasis is encapsulated in the phrase "a crown of life." That is not merely a future reward, but is a gift for this life. It is a state of being—a manner of living that ought to describe all believers. It is what we might call "really living." James uses these terms to describe the state of the person who does not give up when confronted with difficulties, but who, in fact, rejoices in the wisdom of God . . . and remains steadfastly faithful to the God who loves them.

A dear friend of ours, in the backlash of her dad's very sudden death, expressed the perspective James is after, in a letter she wrote me after the funeral:

Thank you for going "above and beyond the call of duty" in helping us with Dad's memorial service. The service was really a praise service, wasn't it? About half of those attending don't know Christ as Lord, and we were thrilled that they heard such a clear explanation of the Gospel. We have heard that people at APS are still talking about the service, and many have asked for a copy of the tape! From my angle, the discussion of Dad having eternal life and a mansion prepared just for him—*what a comfort!*

We are all coping, but missing Dad more each day. I think it gets harder before it gets easier. The reality of death is very hard to grasp—even now I can't quite believe my Dad is gone. For the last thirty-one years he has always been there. I think it hits bit by bit—not all at once, as that would be overwhelming. The call from Mom saying he was gone, seeing Dad at St. Joe's, the memorial service, packing up his office, my birthday party without his name on the card, his absence at church on Sunday—event by event it slowly sinks in— he's not here. Heaven has never been so real, or so looked forward to, as it is now.

Your continued prayers for my mom are appreciated. Your sermon this past Sunday was a real encouragement for her. Thank you!

Thank you for the card and kind note I received today. Give Patricia my love and thanks too.

Under His Wing,
Becky

Be patient, therefore, brethren, until the coming of the Lord.
Behold, the farmer waits for the precious produce
of the soil, being patient about it, until it gets
the early and the late rains.
You too be patient; strengthen your hearts,
for the coming of the Lord is at hand.

Do not complain, brethren, against one another,
that you yourselves may not be judged; behold,
the Judge is standing right at the door.

As an example, brethren, of suffering and patience,
take the prophets who spoke in the name of the Lord.
Behold, we count those blessed who endured.
You have heard of the endurance of Job and have
seen the outcome of the Lord's dealings, that the
Lord is full of compassion and is merciful.

James 5:7-11

9

When You Have to Keep Going

Georgi Vins was released from a Russian prison in June of 1979, after spending almost fifteen years in prison, three at hard labor. He was completing his fifth year of a five-year sentence, which was to be followed by five years of exile in Siberia. Suddenly he was given a suit, a shirt, a tie and told that he was being stripped of his Soviet citizenship. Within forty-eight hours he found himself in the United States.

As you learn of his family history, you discover that his mother, at the age of sixty-eight, was arrested and sentenced to three years in prison for aiding Christians. Georgi was only seven years old the last time he saw his father, who died in prison. Sometime ago he was being interviewed by Bill Moyers on public television.

"Your father died in prison," Moyers recalled. "Your mother was arrested. You've spent much of your life in prison. You once wrote, 'Our life has not been given for empty dreaming.' What has yours meant? What do you think your lives signify?"

His reply was to the point, "I do not regret the years I have spent, even the years of suffering. *This has been the purpose of my living.*"

Her name is Lois Gray. She has developed a very fragile

immune system through her work in chemical laboratories in a hospital. Today she is literally allergic to her general environment.

You hand her a towel, but she cannot wipe her hands because she is allergic to the detergent that was used to wash the towel. She goes to a hotel, but she cannot sleep on the mattress because she is allergic to synthetics. She has to go outside and lie on the veranda, if there is one, or on the floor outside the room, because she's allergic to the synthetics in the rug. She has to bring her own food, because she's allergic to the preservatives which are used in nearly every food we eat. She rarely has four good days in a row . . . but when she does, she manages to smile.[1]

Had we sat where Georgi Vins sat or walked with Lois Gray, I wonder if our response to suffering would have been the same. We tend to think in isolated terms, to view our own circumstances as unique, as more intense and pressurized than anyone else's. And this causes us to respond inappropriately.

James understood that cycle, and so before he brought the letter to a close, he shifted gears. Over the last several chapters, he was very intensely invading our private space and exposing our raw edges. He wrestled each of us to the mat in an attempt to get us to see the weaknesses of our Christian life.

But now in the middle of chapter 5, he removes the cloak of the confronting prophet and puts on the robe of a comforting pastor and friend to address three pressing problems in our lives. He talks about Christian friends who wander from the faith. He looks into the reflection of our lives and shares some insights on the subject of sickness and sin. And he returns to the theme he began the book with, as he walks with us through the heat of our suffering and opposition.

In this section James is urging us not to fight back in a revengeful spirit at those who assault us. He calls us to patience with people. But he also pleads with us to endure the trying circumstances of life that confront us ... and leave us without answers. He so intently wants to communicate this that he resorts to repeating himself. Four times he uses the term *patience,* and twice he talks about *endurance.* His theme is "Our Patient Endurance in the Face of Life's Extremities."

SUFFERING

One of those extremities is seen in the word *suffering.* It is found in James 5:10:

> As an example, brethren, of suffering and patience, take the prophets who spoke in the name of the Lord.

The word *suffering* means "to bear hardship, to suffer misfortune, to endure affliction." James mentions it as a characteristic of the life of the Old Testament prophets. His point is that even God's most eminent servants in the past were not exempt from tragedy. Although God honored them by using them as His spokesmen, they did not escape horrible difficulties in their lives. Rather, it seems that their very work provoked opposition. We see this particularly in Hebrews 11:

> And what more shall I say? For time will fail me
> if I tell of Gideon, Barak, Samson, Jephthah,
> of David and Samuel and the prophets (v. 32).

From there the author outlines some of the high points in the lives of these prophets, but that is not all he mentions. The dark side of their lives is captured as well:

> Women received back their dead by resurrection;
> and others were tortured, not accepting their release,
> in order that they might obtain a better resurrection;
> and others experienced mockings and scourgings,
> yes, also chains and imprisonment. They were stoned,
> they were sawn in two, they were tempted,

they were put to death with the sword;
they went about in sheepskins, in goatskins,
being destitute, afflicted, ill-treated
(men of whom the world was not worthy),
wandering in deserts and mountains
and caves and holes in the ground (vv. 35-38).

It is that part of the prophet's job description that James is referring to with the word *suffering*. Although he speaks of the prophets as a group, there is a prophet who stands out as one who endured incredible mistreatment. His name is Jeremiah, but his nickname, "the Weeping Prophet," betrays the pain he endured. His task from God was to proclaim a series of messages to his friends from God. His friends took offense at the sternness of the messages and turned against him. As a result, Jeremiah was put in prison, then in stocks, and finally into a miry dungeon. Listen to Jeremiah's own version of his struggle, as recorded in the *International Children's Bible:*

> I tell the people about the message I received from the Lord, but this only brings me insults. The people make fun of me all day long. . . . I hear many people whispering about me: "Terror on every side! Let's tell the rulers about him." My friends are all just waiting for me to make some mistake. They are saying, "Maybe we can trick Jeremiah. Then we can defeat him. Then we can pay him back." But the Lord is with me like a strong warrior.[2]

When James talks about enduring suffering, Jeremiah would have come to his mind. Would we? At this moment, you may be undergoing incredible difficulties, suffering endlessly, with no relief on the horizon. Yet you endure it, like Jeremiah. You would have come to his mind. But some Christians would not, because they have attempted to theologically remove themselves from suffering so that they do not view it as acceptable. Or, having suffered, they have assumed that it is some sort of divine vendetta being enacted on them for their sin. Or worse, some sort of cosmic joke.

PATIENCE

James speaks to us about patient endurance in life's extremities . . . and the extremity of suffering is first. But there is another, which finds its boundaries of definition in verses 7 and 8.

Be patient, therefore, brethren,
until the coming of the Lord.
Behold, the farmer waits for the precious produce of the soil,
being patient about it, until it gets the early and late rains.
You too be patient; strengthen your hearts,
for the coming of the Lord is at hand.

The term *patience* is more involved than our usual definition of the word. It means first of all "to patiently endure." Patience can endure delay and suffering without giving up. In that sense it is the mirror image of the word "suffering."

But it is more than that. Patience describes the attitude of self-restraint that does not try to get even for a wrong that has been suffered. It has as its focus patience with people. One of the best preachers of the fourth century, John Chrysostom, defined patience as "the spirit which could take revenge if it liked, but refuses to do so." Would that describe you? Or do you like to get even? Listen as one writer discusses patience:

Patience is a quality of character that often seems to be in short supply in this modern world. . . . In a world where computers, supersonic jets, and satellite communications create a sense of instancy, we can lose the meaning of patience; we simply don't like to wait for things — or for growth or development in people. We want each other to change, to mature, to respond in certain ways instantly. . . . But sometimes it takes years to develop wisdom, the grace and the endurance we want to see in one another. For such people growth cannot happen outside the environment of patience. Simply put, patience is the willingness to generously give another time and space to grow. . . . Patience does not demand; it waits.[3]

Why is that so hard for us? I think it's because of another shade of emphasis which comes from two Greek words, which literally translated mean "a long way from anger." Patience, then, means "to restrain our tempers." The believer in Jesus Christ is not to allow mistreatment and oppression to drive him to hatred, bitterness, or despair. A patient person attempts to calm a quarrel, by controlling anger and not seeking revenge. Patience is the opposite of being quick-tempered.

That is not our natural tendency, is it? And yet, James encourages us to model it. Instead of allowing ourselves to be weakened by impatience and vindictiveness, we need to move in the direction of our strength. In verse 7, James speaks of the early rains which came in late October and November, assuring the farmer that the seed would begin to grow. The latter rains which came in April and May assured him that the harvest would be good. But between November and May, he would have to wait. You know that after he plants the seed, the farmer does not go out each day and dig it up to see if it is growing. Nor does he replant it somewhere else where the conditions might be more favorable. He waits because he knows that the value of the harvest, the end product, is worth waiting for.

James' point to his Christian friends is much the same. We are assured over and over in Scripture that Christ will return to this planet as King and Judge. When He does, He will put an end to all opposition and will make suffering a thing of the past. That is what we wait for. That is what is to give us strength to go on.

Joe Bayly expresses how we feel in a piece he entitled,

"A Psalm While Packing Books:"

This cardboard box
Lord
see it says
Bursting limit
200 lbs. per square inch.
The box maker knew
how much strain
the box would take
what weight
would crush it.
You are wiser
than the box maker
Maker of my spirit
my mind
my body.
Does the box know
when pressure increases close to
the limit?
No
it knows nothing.
But I know
when my breaking point
is near.
And so I pray
Maker of my soul
Determiner of the pressure
within
upon me
Stop it
lest I be broken
or else
change the pressure rating
of this fragile container
of Your grace
so that I may bear more.[4]

I believe with all my heart that our God knows our limit.
But I also believe that most of us have set our limit far too

low. James is suggesting that it can be raised as we find a renewed strength in the hope of the second coming of Jesus Christ. In fact, the verb *strengthen* in verse 8 conveys the idea of "supporting something so that it will stand firm and unmoving." Instead of being constantly agitated and shaken by our experiences, we need to develop an inner sense of stability. The Williams' paraphrase of the New Testament puts it this way, "You must put iron into your hearts."

This kind of strength is only to be found in our personal hope of Christ's return. If that hope is relegated to such a remote and distant future that it has no present impact on our way of living, then this great Christian doctrine no longer exercises the vital strengthening influence upon our day-to-day experiences that James says it should.

Suffering reveals our creature status. We are not all wise or infinite in strength, but God is. We need Him desperately, and sometimes it takes coming to the end of ourselves to see that. But when that does occur—when the hinges on life start to fall off, when it seems like the room is closing in all around us—this doctrine of the Second Coming is designed to give us strength because God's purpose will be accomplished in us.

When children are allowed to do what they like and are constantly shielded from situations in which their feelings might get hurt, we describe them as spoiled. When we say that, we mean that overindulgent parenthood not only makes them unattractive today but also fails to prepare them for the moral demands of adult life tomorrow—two evils for the price of one. But God, who always has His eye on tomorrow as He deals with us today, never spoils His children; and the lifelong training course in holy living in which He enrolls us challenges and tests us to the utmost again and again. Christlike habits of action and reaction—in other words, the fruit of the Spirit, are ingrained most deeply as we learn to maintain them through experiences of pain and unpleasantness, which in retrospect appear as God's chisel for sculpting our souls.[5]

Bill Butterworth illustrates this truth beautifully. Read on.

Kids are great teachers. This happened a while ago, but the lesson lingered.

My wife finds great enjoyment and fulfillment in needlework. She's most content curled up in a cozy chair, creating with crewel or counted cross-stitch.

One night, as Rhonda was working on her project, I overhead Jeffrey contribute his own editorial comment on Mama's craft.

"Mama, that pitcher looks yukky!"

I thought that was a pretty harsh critique coming from the mouth of a two-year-old. I looked up at him, ready to reprove him when I noticed his perspective on the issue.

He was staring at the back of the needlework.

Living life down there among the two-year-olds, Jeffrey was not able to see the front of the picture, as any adult could with ease. To him needlework was a tangle of knots, loose threads, and disjointed strings with no apparent order or purpose.

It was then that Rhonda turned over the picture so that Jeffrey could see the real project.

"Oh, that's nice, Mama! It's so pity!" (That's two-year-old talk for "It's so pretty!")

Once he saw it from the right perspective, it became beautiful in his little eyes.

Many of us are faced with similar circumstances in our Christian lives. God has put us through some things that can best be described by the word *yukky*.

As we look at these times of trial in our lives, it's easy to take the child's perspective. Life can look pretty tangled and disjointed from the human side.

But remember, we are God's handiwork.

He is creating within us a beautiful needlework. During the time of endurance, it's important to remember that the result is greater resemblance to His character.

For there will come a point in time when God will turn over His needlework in order for us to see the beauty, order, and purpose to His work in our lives.

It's a whole different picture from God's perspective.

Just as kids don't always understand the adult perspective, humans don't always understand the work of God.[6]

COMPLAINING AND JUDGING

One possible response to suffering is that we start *complaining* and *judging* others.

Do not complain, brethren, against one another, that you yourselves may not be judged; behold, the Judge is standing right at the door (v. 9).

The word *complain* speaks primarily of inner distress. And what James is cautioning us about is our unexpressed but very real feelings of bitterness or resentment because of the pain that we are forced to endure. Those feelings, if not dealt with, will not remain unexpressed but will bubble to the surface and find expression in a number of ways.

Most do not fully see this truth that life is difficult. Instead they moan more or less incessantly, noisily or subtly, about the enormity of their problems, their burdens, and their difficulties as if life were generally easy, as if life *should* be easy. They voice their belief, noisily or subtly, that their difficulties represent a unique kind of affliction that should not be and that has somehow been especially visited upon them, or else upon their families, their tribe, their class, their nation, their race or even their species, and not upon others. I know about this moaning because I have done my share.[7]

Perhaps there is another way this marks our lives and

that is through *criticism* and *faultfinding* of others. But here's the sad part of this — that expression usually hits those closest to us who very often have nothing to do with the problem. The warning here is against our natural tendency — when subjected to pressure and suffering — to give vent to our frustrations by lashing out against those near and dear to us. One commentator observed:

> Here are Christians under severe pressure and beginning to fray at the edges. So often the first people to suffer when we begin to crack under the strain are our fellow Christians. "Divide and conquer" is one of Satan's favorite tactics. One of the greatest things he can do to advance his purposes is to cause division among Christians, to make them complain, murmur, fight, bicker and quarrel with each other.[8]

James is saying, "Look, don't let the pressure that is brought to bear on you from the outside push you to be un-Christian with each other on the inside." What often happens is that we start to blame our friends, or those closest to us, for the troubles that are consuming us. That accomplishes nothing.

> Blame never affirms, it assaults.
> Blame never restores, it wounds.
> Blame never solves, it complicates.
> Blame never unites, it separates.
> Blame never smiles, it frowns.
> Blame never forgives, it rejects.
> Blame never forgets, it remembers.
> Blame never builds, it destroys.[9]

That's why we must be careful in our response to suffering. We tend to say things we shouldn't. Now for many of us, that is enough of a warning to be careful. But for some, more is needed. That is why he adds:

> Do not complain, brethren, against one another, that you yourselves may not be judged; behold, the Judge is standing right at the door (v. 9).

As believers looking forward to the Second Coming, we anticipate the end of suffering and injustice. James is warning us here that blaming one another for our suffering and pain places us in danger of judgment from Christ when He returns.

The nearness of the second coming of Christ offers us great strength, but also serves as a reminder to examine our own behavior in the face of suffering.

ENDURANCE AND TRUST

There are two other possible responses to suffering. They stand together and really undergird much of what we've already seen. But James articulates both of them for us in verse 11:

> Behold, we count those blessed who endured. You have heard of the endurance of Job and have seen the outcome of the Lord's dealings, that the Lord is full of compassion and is merciful.

Endurance does not easily break under suffering. In the Gospels, the word is translated "to stay on in the same place." Endurance is to stay in there when you'd like to run away. But it doesn't occur in a vacuum. Endurance is the active determination of a believer whose faith triumphs in the midst of afflictions. That's what made Job unforgettable. In one frightening hour he lost all his real estate investments, his livestock holdings, and his family. Now as you read the account of Job's life, you see him sometimes very angry for what has happened to him. At other times, he abruptly questions the advice of his so-called friends and even agonizes over the terrible thought that God might have deserted him. But the great part of his story is that in spite of the agonizing questions that tore at his heart, *he never lost his faith in God and determined to endure.*

In *The Complete Book of Running,* the late Jim Fixx

describes what he learned about endurance:

> When we race, strange things happen to our minds.
> The stress of fatigue sometimes makes us forget why
> we wanted to race in the first place. In one of my early
> marathons I found myself unable to think of a single
> reason for continuing. Physically and mentally ex-
> hausted, I dropped out of the race. Now I won't enter
> a marathon unless I truly want to finish it. If during
> the race I can't remember why I wanted to run in it, I
> tell myself, "Maybe I can't remember now, but I know
> I had a good reason when I started. . . ."[10]

A spirit of endurance will remind us that our suffering is
not purposeless, that it is not simply pain inflicted for the
sake of pain. . . . that it is not the result of a Deity who has
lost control, but that, in fact, it is moving us toward a goal.
In that we must rest, in an abiding trust in God's methods.
We see at the end of verse 11 that "the Lord is full of
compassion and is merciful."

The Bible declares that God's purposes for our lives,
even in suffering, are good. James indicates that they are
compassionate and merciful because they flow out of the
character of our God who does not make mistakes.

But please keep in mind that our appreciation of that
good may not come until after the suffering is over. The
word translated as "outcome" in verse 11 tells us that. It
means "the finished product, the conclusion." It indicates
the goal or purpose toward which something is moving.

I am sure Job did not see the compassionate purpose of
God's dealing in his life while he was staring into the teeth
of his suffering. It wasn't until after the situation was over,
the trial past, that Job saw that God's dealings were in fact
compassionate and merciful. Insight often comes after the
suffering, when we begin to see it from God's vantage
point.

In the meantime, our challenge is to patiently endure,
and to avoid the all-too-easy tendency to complain and

blame others for our problems. We do this as we find strength and stability in the hope of Christ's second coming, and trust in the wonderful person of our God right now.

A young preacher was in his first appointment, and the challenges and problems of that parish raised so many doubts within his mind that they really undermined his faith. He would have been lost had he not met Grandma Sudley. Grandma Sudley gave him life. Let me tell his story as though it were mine.

I used to visit Grandma Sudley when I wanted to get away from the complaints and troubles of the congregation. I would pretend to be making calls on shut-ins, but I was really going to be with a friend.

"How are your ladies?" she would always ask.

And I would always respond, "They're still after me."

"Not me," she would say. She always asked me to pray for her, even though we both knew that she prayed more frequently and more powerfully than I did. It was her way of affirming me and letting me know she needed me.

Then came the day I received the word that she was dying and her family wanted me to come see her. I went with fear and trembling because I knew that if she was dying, I was losing my greatest friend, the greatest minister to me. When I got there, the family was clutched together, and the nurse came and said, "She'll see you now, Preacher."

"Me?" I asked.

"You're the pastor, aren't you?" I had to go, even though I didn't want to go. I felt so inadequate and alone and weak and sad. They had a tube in her nose and other tubes in her arms, and all I could say was, "God, help me." I kept hoping she wouldn't wake up, and I stood away from the bed.

Then she stirred, opened her eyes and saw me. She smiled and said teasingly, "How are your ladies?"

I tried to smile, but there was silence for a long

time as I held her hand. It was soft and at the same time hard—bony and brittle.

After a while, she looked at me again and said, "I guess I'm going to leave."

"I know," I said.

"I'm very tired."

"I know."

Then she smiled again and said, "I've never died before."

I responded, "I've never been with anyone who died before."

She said, "We're both gonna make it, Preacher. Would you listen to me while I pray?" It was her final affirmation of me, because she knew I couldn't pray in that moment. And she began to pray, "O Father, take me home to be with Jesus. And protect this boy of mine. He's been a good pastor to me. He has loved me and meant so much to me. Protect him. Amen."

I was crying, but she said, "It's all right. It's going to be all right, Preacher. We're going to make it. You tell the people out there we're going to make it."

"I'll tell them, Grandma, I'll tell them."

She closed her eyes and fell asleep, and that was the last time I saw her alive.

Sometimes when I drive by that cemetery out there in the country where we buried Grandma Sudley, even though it's hot and I'm sweaty and I'm running out of time, I stop the car and think about Grandma Sudley. And I thank God for a woman who trusted God so completely, who loved Jesus so deeply, that she could make a preacher out of me. I look at her grave across the hill, and I say to her, "We made it, Grandma. We made it."

Grandma Sudley made it. And that young preacher who is one of the most noted preachers in America today made it because he learned it from her.[11]

In this you greatly rejoice, even though now for a little while,
if necessary, you have been distressed by various trials,
that the proof of your faith, being more precious than
gold which is perishable, even though tested by fire,
may be found to result in praise and glory and honor
at the revelation of Jesus Christ;

And though you have not seen Him, you love Him, and though
you do not see Him now, but believe in Him,
you greatly rejoice with joy inexpressible
and full of glory, obtaining as the outcome of
your faith the salvation of your souls.

As to this salvation, the prophets who prophesied of the
grace that would come to you made careful search and
inquiry, seeking to know what person or time the
Spirit of Christ within them was indicating as He
predicted the sufferings of Christ and the glories
to follow. It was revealed to them that they were
not serving themselves, but you, in these things
which now have been announced to you through
those who preached the gospel to you by the Holy
Spirit sent from heaven — things into which
angels long to look.

1 Peter 1:6-12

10
When the Heat Is On

In the movie, *The Hiding Place*, there is a scene set in the Ravensbruck concentration camp in Germany, where Corrie ten Boom and her sister, Betsie, are, along with 10,000 other women, in degrading conditions. In this scene, the two are gathered with some of the women in the barracks in the midst of the beds, cold and hungry and lice-ridden, and Betsie is leading a Bible class. One of the other women calls out derisively from her bunk and mocks their worship of God. They fall into conversation, and this woman says what so frequently is flung at Christians, "If your God is such a good God, why does He allow this kind of suffering?" Dramatically she tears off the bandages and old rags that bind her hands, displaying her broken, mangled fingers and says, "I'm the first violinist of the symphony orchestra. Did your God will this?"

For a moment no one answers. Then Corrie ten Boom steps to the side of her sister and says, "We can't answer that question. All we know is that our God came to this earth, and became one of us, and He suffered with us and was crucified and died. And that He did it for love."[1]

It was supposed to be like any other two-week period of time in my life, but it turned out to be like no other two weeks I can remember. It began with the suicide of a prominent church member and successful businessman and his subsequent funeral which over 600 people attended. It included the confession of a forty-three-year-old man who murdered his father when he was thirteen. It continued at lunch with a dear friend and businessman who told me how he had made $30 million in three years, and in the space of a few weeks had lost it. It focused on a Christian friend who had loaned $70,000 to another Christian — money to be paid back in seven days, but the guy walked. While I was on the phone taking the police report regarding the suicide, I received a long-distance call from a pastor friend in another state, informing me that after just fourteen months in his new church, he had been fired.[2]

It is in days like these that we look down at the fuel gauge and see it is reading close to empty. And even as we hear the engine sputtering, we can't help but wish we had never learned how to drive. If you doubt that, just ask Peter. He knew what it was like to feel the vice of pain tighten ever so slowly around him. Sometimes it was his own fault, but not all the time. In fact, as you track his life through the Book of Acts, you discover that Peter, although enjoying great fame and prominence, also knew what it was like to suffer. . . . alone. That's why his heart leaped to those who were in the wringer. He sensed their anguish, he felt their despair. And the more their pain shouted, the more Peter had to write to them, to try to ease the load. And that's what he did in the New Testament book we call 1 Peter. His primary purpose was to offer encouragement and hope to suffering Christians. And at that time throughout the Roman Empire, Christians were being forced to scatter from their hometowns and find other places to live.

As a result, loneliness invaded like a cold fog and engulfed them. Then, cutting through their loneliness like a knife, came painful circumstances and the monster of fear.

TRIALS

In this you greatly rejoice, even though now for a little while, if necessary, you have been distressed by various trials (v. 6).

The word *distressed* is actually a military term meaning "to be harassed." It describes inner mental distress or sadness because of difficult circumstances. It is a word that we are familiar with, just as we are with the "various trials" in verse 6. The word *various* means "multicolored, diverse." Whatever pressure or pain you could imagine, whatever shape, size or color, they were experiencing it. As you may be. Five or six years ago when you were pushed to the wall with pain, you figured that there was nothing else that could intercept your life and sabotage your dreams. But that was before this year; what you could not have imagined for your life has now come true. So you're familiar with the word "various trials."

Now, just in case you wonder about your pain, your suffering, just in case you imagine that it is worse than anyone else's, let me acquaint you with the pain that Peter's readers were experiencing.

It is likely that the incredible persecution led by the Roman Emperor Nero had begun. In that persecution, Christians were wrapped in freshly slaughtered animal skins and fed to dogs and wild animals. They were dipped in pitch or tar and set on fire as torches to light Nero's gardens at night. That persecution was the first of nine that took place in the Roman Empire over the next 250 years. Both Peter and Paul died in this first persecution.

My friends, we must realize that affliction is something

we all need to deal with. In fact, persecution and affliction are a normal part of the Christian life. Scott Peck opens his brilliant best-seller *The Road Less Traveled,* with the statement, "Life is difficult," and then continues:

> This is a great truth, one of the greatest truths. It is a great truth because once we truly see this truth, we transcend it. Once we truly know that life is difficult, then life is no longer difficult. Because once it has been accepted, the fact that life is difficult no longer matters.[3]

TRIALS THAT REFINE US

Living the Christian life is a battle, not a picnic. It always involves conflict and pressure, and you don't seem to find much R & R. Then your world begins to unravel even more, and you say, "Lord, I'm unemployed . . . I've just gone bankrupt . . . or I've just gone through a fortune . . . I've just lost the company . . . I've just lost my home."

But the Lord says, "I know. I count you worthy for the kingdom of God . . . and that is why you are suffering." We're not talking about bad judgment on earth. We're not talking about a stupid decision made in heaven. We're talking about pressure and hardship and difficulty, for it is those things that refine us. And that is precisely how Peter calls it in verse 7:

> That the proof of your faith, being more precious than gold which is perishable, even though tested by fire, may be found to result in praise and glory and honor at the revelation of Jesus Christ.

Certainly, feelings of being crushed, overwhelmed, devastated and torn wash over those who suffer, and Peter does not disregard those emotions, but he does move past them to describe some of the results of trials in our lives . . . the elements of refining.

Verse 7 talks about "the proof of your faith" or "the genuineness of your faith" being proven by trials or tests. We need to remember that the followers of God in both the Old and the New Testaments knew that God would use their trying circumstances to test their hearts and their lives in order to mature them spiritually. In other words, it is through difficulties that God checks whether our faith is genuine.

In verse 7, Peter uses the work of a goldsmith to illustrate what he's talking about. You see, mining is only the first step in a process that converts gold into a useful product. To form an object, that gold must be cast into a mold. Now gold doesn't melt until almost 1900 degrees Fahrenheit, at which point the impurities rise to the surface and are burned off. The smith knows the gold is ready to cast when the surface of the liquid becomes mirrorlike and he can see his face in it.

Let's look at the parallel in our lives. In the refining process, it can get awfully hot; but the hotter it gets, the more we grow spiritually, the more we become like Jesus Christ and reflect His character. Peter is reminding us that if we are going to follow Christ, we must follow Him in all aspects of life . . . the good and the bad, the painful and the joyful. Trials test our faith, but out of them our faith can emerge stronger, clearer, and firmer than ever before.

If we think of trials in terms of the training that an athlete undergoes, we know that training is not meant to make him collapse, but to enable him to develop more strength and staying power. Pain, affliction, and suffering are not meant to take strength out of us, but to put strength into us.

In verse 6, Peter says that we go through various or multicolored trials. He uses that word only one other time in this letter, in verse 10 of chapter 4, and there he describes the grace of God as being "varied or manifold." Here's the connection. Our difficulties may be multicolored, but so is the grace of God. There is nothing in the human situation which the grace of God cannot match. Whatever life is doing to us, the grace of God enables us to meet and overcome. There is a grace to match every trial — and there is no trial without its grace.

When God permits us to go through the furnace, He keeps His eye on the clock and His hand on the thermostat. If we rebel, He may have to reset the clock; but if we submit, He will not permit us to suffer one minute too long. Trials then, should not surprise us or cause us to continually doubt God's faithfulness. In fact, lurking beneath the surface of these verses is the flip side of what we've just talked about: *The faith that does not endure under suffering cannot be acclaimed as genuine.* Through the difficulties of life God tests our faith in order to prove its sincerity. A faith that cannot be tested cannot be trusted. People who throw in the towel when the going gets tough are demonstrating that they really had no faith at all.

In his book *On the Anvil,* Max Lucado writes about the hammering we seem to take so regularly:

In the shop of a blacksmith, there are three types of tools. There are tools on the junkpile: outdated, broken, dull, rusty. They sit in the cobwebbed corner, useless to their master, oblivious to their calling.

There are tools on the anvil: melted down, molten hot, moldable, changeable. They lie on the anvil, being shaped by their master, accepting their calling.

There are tools of usefulness: sharpened, primed, defined, mobile. They lie ready in the blacksmith's tool chest, available to their master, fulfilling their calling.

Some people lie useless: lives broken, talents wasting, fires quenched, dreams dashed. They are tossed in with the scrap iron, in desperate need of repair, with no notion of purpose.

Others lie on the anvil: hearts open, hungry to change, wounds healing, vision clearing. They welcome the painful pounding of the blacksmith's hammer, longing to be rebuilt, begging to be called.

Others lie in their Master's hands; well-tuned, noncompromising, polished, productive. They respond to their Master's forearm, demanding nothing, surrendering all.

We are all somewhere in the blacksmith's shop. we are either on the scrap pile, on the anvil, in the Master's hands, or in the tool chest.[4]

TRIALS THAT PREPARE US

There's another result of trials. It's not one that shows up right away; in fact, it may be some time before we see it.

That the proof of your faith, being more precious than gold which is perishable, even though tested by fire, may be found to result in praise and glory and honor at the revelation of Jesus Christ (v. 7).

The faith of these Christians had met with scoffing, rejection, pain, and persecution on earth. But when the Lord returns, Peter says, the scene will be reversed. Our trying experiences today are preparing us for glory tomorrow. When Christ returns and we see Him, we will bring "praise and glory and honor" to Him if we have been faithful in the sufferings of this life. Furthermore, we will receive praise and honor from Him.

Peter reminds us that God's purposes in our present grief may not be fully understood in a week, in a year, or even in a lifetime. In fact, some of God's purposes will not be known when believers die and go to be with the Lord. Some will be discovered only at the day of final judgment when the Lord reveals the secrets of all hearts and commends with special honor those who trusted Him in hardship even though they could not see the reason for the pain. They trusted Him simply because He was their God and they knew Him to be worthy of trust.

God, it is drastically important
That the pain of this past year
Is not wasted.
How tragic it would be
To suffer so much
And gain so little.
What I *must* learn in my pain
Is that it is always leading
To something far beyond
What I can see in the shadows.
I *must* learn that You are not reckless
Or careless or cruel.
You are *for* me, and always
In some way, at some time
There is Your "nevertheless afterward."
I *must* learn that there is never a moment
When You are not worthy of praise.
Bad things happen
But there is only goodness in You.
I *must* learn that when my heart is broken
You are able to break my impatience, my pride
My carelessness and selfishness.
All of this I *must* learn.
O God, teach me well . . . teach me well.
It is drastically important
That the pain is not wasted.[5]

Sue Holtcamp, wrote a fantastic article in *Decision* Magazine of April 1985. She tells of having a life that was almost untouched. She credited it to the fact that God protects His own. Then it started caving in — seven hospitalizations . . . three back surgeries in three years . . . drug dependency for the pain.

After twenty years of building a business, her husband lost it all. This drove him to a clear personal relationship with Jesus Christ.

"You know," she said, "one night I was talking to our seventeen-year-old daughter, Katie. As she spoke about Jesus, she ended up making this statement, 'All I know about Him—and I know it for certain—is that I love and I trust Jesus Christ.' Under her breath she said, 'I may never know anything more.' "

The next day Sue saw her daughter and her husband take off in a private plane. Shortly after it was out of sight, the plane disintegrated.

"Half my family was dead," she observed, "and I wondered if I could bear it. By the grace of God I could, because of Jesus."[6]

OUR RESPONSE TO TRIALS

The final thing Peter wants us to consider, when the heat is on, is *our personal response* to trials. Our consistent response to pain, to alienation, to suffering, to fear, to persecution should be *love* and *belief*.

> And though you have not seen Him, you love Him, and though you do not see Him now, but believe in Him, you greatly rejoice with joy inexpressible and full of glory (v. 8).

The vast majority of Peter's readers had no personal contact with Christ while He lived on this earth, but that did not handicap them spiritually. By accepting the testimony of those who had seen Christ, they entered into a personal relationship with Him. They chose to *love* Him and to *believe* in Him.

The word *believe* as used here means "to trust or rest your confidence in someone, to depend on them." It has the idea of resting yourself in Christ. It's one thing to believe in Jesus Christ as your personal Savior from sin, and we all must do that. But it is yet another thing to depend on Him, to trust Him when everything around you seems to be coming apart.

Why is that so important? You know the answer, because you remember Peter. Everybody remembers Peter. Men-

tion his name in a group of people who really don't know
the Bible, and someone will be able to pull from the shelf
of memory the story of a guy named Peter and a rooster . . .
and a denial. Everybody remembers Peter. And Peter remembered that story too. He would never forget it. He,
who lived and breathed Christ for three years, in the greatest moment of crisis denied that One. And he wants to
spare us the pain of such an experience by challenging us
to love and to trust even in the most difficult of circumstances. Remember how A.W. Tozer said it?

> What we need very badly these days is a company of
> Christians who are *prepared to trust God* as complete-
> ly now as they know they must do at the last day. For
> each of us, the time is surely coming when we shall
> have nothing but God . . . To the man of pseudo faith
> that is a terrifying thought, but to real faith, it is one of
> the most comforting thoughts the heart can entertain.[7]

Not only are we to evidence love and belief . . . but also
joy. The word *rejoice* in verse 8 refers to an outward or
external expression of joy. It reflects out of a heart that is
thankful to God for who He is and for what He has provided us through our salvation — great joy because of God's
grace and mercy.

As the people to whom Peter wrote thought about their
hope in heaven, they continually rejoiced even though the
pain was great. You see, hope should lead to joy. Remember that rejoicing is not a continual feeling of hilarity, nor is
it a denial of pain and anguish. That's not it at all. Instead,
it is an anticipatory joy experienced even now, despite our
circumstances, because as believers we know that our
sufferings are only for "a little while," and our hope is for
eternity.

We would like this "little while" to be confined to six or
seven minutes or perhaps a couple of days; but throughout
the history of the church, many Christians have suffered for
years. Peter is telling us that no matter how long our suffer-

ing lasts, it is nothing in light of eternity. And although those trials may cause temporary grief, they still cannot extinguish that deep, abiding joy which is galvanized to our hope in Jesus Christ.

Fullness of joy comes when there is a deep sense of the presence of God in your life. Jesus made it clear, as does Peter, that joy is inseparably connected to love and trust, and that there can be joy in suffering when it is seen to have a redemptive purpose. That is why biblical joy does not depend on circumstances. In fact, it is cited most frequently in the Scripture as existing in spite of our circumstances.

That joy begins to form in our lives as we become connected to Jesus Christ by faith. That's when our hope begins to bloom. And that joy is something that even the Old Testament prophets and angels of heaven longed to participate in.

> As to this salvation, the prophets who prophesied of the grace that would come to you made careful search and inquiry, seeking to know what person or time the Spirit of Christ within them was indicating as He predicted the sufferings of Christ and the glories to follow.
>
> It was revealed to them that they were not serving themselves, but you, in these things which now have been announced to you through those who preached the gospel to you by the Holy Spirit sent from heaven — things into which angels long to look (vv. 10-12).

The prophets who wrote the Old Testament longed to participate in this salvation and future period of grace, and tried to discover when it would all come together. And the reality of the Christian's living hope was even held in awe and wonder by the angels in heaven.

As these Old Testament prophets wrote, they often did not understand the full significance of their words, especially as they wrote about the coming Messiah. But they thought about it, searched the subject out as best they could, and discovered that the Messiah would have to suffer first. . . . and then glory would follow. And that is the pattern for our lives.

> Our suffering is not a sign that Christ has betrayed us, or that He is no longer Lord; rather it is a sign of our fellowship with the risen Lord who first suffered for us. Suffering, indeed, becomes a sign of the glory which is to follow (for us).[8]

We can't answer all the questions! But we know what Corrie ten Boom knew, that "our God came to this earth, and became one of us, and He suffered with us and was crucified and died. And that He did it for love."

One glorious day we'll be able to talk to Him about that, and about all our unanswered questions.

And we know that God causes all things to work together for good to those who love God, to those who are called according to His purpose. For whom He foreknew, He also predestined to become conformed to the image of His Son, that He might be the first-born among many brethren; and whom He predestined, these He also called; and whom He called, these He also justified; and whom He justified, these He also glorified.

Romans 8:28-30

11
When God
Lets You Fall

Twenty-year-old David Koop was a mountain-climbing enthusiast. It was what he enjoyed doing the most in his leisure time. But while on a springtime climb in the mountains of New Hampshire several years ago, David was struck by a huge falling rock. The impact caused him to slip from the steep mountainside and hurtle down to the valley floor. His climbing partner, to whom he was attached by rope, dug into the mountainside and clung there desperately, watching in horror as his friend fell . . . until the rope ran out of slack, tightened and jerked the falling David Koop to an abrupt stop in mid-air . . . killing him instantly.

David was the loved son of his parents, Dr. and. Mrs. C. Everett Koop. Dr. Koop, our country's former Surgeon General, has saved the lives of countless children. He has operated on babies in great need, giving them years of life in place of the imminent death they were facing. But he could not save his own son. He could not even help him.

David was a believer in Jesus Christ and in active service for Him. The Bible he left behind, when he was so suddenly taken from his family and the others who needed him, was marked in such a way that his family knew the last verse he had read before going on that climb. His Bible was open to verse 24 of the Book of Jude, which reads, "Now unto Him who is able to *keep you from falling,* and to present you faultless before the presence of His glory with exceeding joy."[1]

The God who could have kept David Koop from fall-ing . . . *did not.* And if you are like me, you wonder *why not?*

The problem of God's care for us, on the one hand, and the difficulties of life that seem to assault us without warn-ing, on the other hand, are hard to reconcile. This problem is most acute when your friends succeed . . . but you fail, when other marriages seem to be strong and vibrant . . . but yours is collapsing before your eyes, when other sons and daughters mature and develop without major-league prob-lems . . . but yours create only pain and grief, when Chris-tian acquaintances seem to sail through life . . . but you stumble with the incredible burden of emotional problems that *won't* go away.

At such times it is difficult to reconcile God's care with our pain. They don't seem to be from the same puzzle. We want to know why God lets it happen to us, and frankly, some verses from the Bible just seem to make the puzzle more confused. The Apostle Paul made just such a state-ment, quoting from Psalm 44, "For thy sake we are being put to death all day long; we were considered as sheep to be slaughtered" (Romans 8:36).

He is talking about how bad it can sometimes get — as though we are going to the slaughterhouse. The same God who makes promises about our protection, about caring for us and meeting our needs now seems to be preoccupied.

In our most transparent moments, each of us would ad-mit that we have struggled with this. God doesn't often explain Himself, and many times is completely silent. It is at those times that Romans 8:28-30 must be our anchor, because it contains, in part, God's answer to our suffering. In many ways, these verses form a summary conclusion to all we've considered in these chapters.

It has been said that there is always an easy solution to every human problem—neat, plausible and *wrong!* Paul does not give us any wrong information in these verses. At the same time, he does not answer all of our questions, but he still does a marvelous job of helping us through the difficult times.

THE PERSON IN CONTROL

Paul begins by reminding us of who is in control when we are out of control. Notice the first part of verse 28, "And we know that God causes all things . . . " The *New International Version* of the Bible puts it in a similar way, "And we know that in all things God works . . . "

The point of this part of the verse is that God is controlling our entire *present* experience, whatever that includes. All of us are facing disappointments and fears right now. So was Paul, even as he wrote these words he was dealing with ridicule, criticism, and alienation.

It is at times like this that we must remember we are not left on God's back burner. In fact, He is superintending our experience because our spiritual development is God's personal commitment. And even in the midst of those aching problems that invade our space, we can *know* that God's hand has not slipped.

In other words, there is no panic in heaven—God is in control. No believer has ever suffered a tragic death without God knowing about it. No businessman has ever failed without God knowing about it. No believer has ever passed over the borderline into mental illness without God knowing it. *We must believe that.* If that is not part and parcel of our perspective, we will never be able to survive suffering in our lives, for that is where we start to struggle. *We want to be in control. We want to determine what comes into our lives.*

Did you know that in the early days of baseball, the

batter signaled the pitcher where to throw the ball? That's right. And the pitcher would hum that ball in there and the batter would hammer it. As the sport evolved, pitching improved and a new pitch was introduced — the curve ball. Then, even if the batter signaled where he wanted it, that curve ball would come in, look great to the last second, and then break away and the batter would miss. The batters hated it because they weren't in control anymore. In our lives, we want to call the pitches, and we want everything right down the middle where we can handle it. But then, God tosses us a curve ball, as it were. We can't handle it . . . and we don't like it. But it is a reminder that God is in control, not us.

GOD'S PROCESS

Within that control is a *process* that God uses.

> And we know that God causes all things to work together for good to those who love God, to those who are called according to His purpose (v. 28).

There are two aspects of the process that we need to consider. First, God *causes all things* to work together, and second, they work together *for good.*

In the first aspect of the process, the verb translated *work together* has several shades of meaning. But the primary sense of the word is "to be a partner in labor, to assist someone as they work." This tells us that God is with us in our difficulties, assisting us as we go through them. He is in control, but He is not off in some black hole in the universe, transcendent and removed, pushing the input buttons on a giant, cosmic computer. He is in control, but He is also at hand to assist.

But notice, also, that our text indicates that God causes *all* things to work together. The word *all* includes all the varied kinds of suffering and afflictions of our lives. It would even include the wrongs inflicted on us by others. It is an all-inclusive word that leaves nothing out.

Paul is not saying that all things are good. You know that is not true. Divorce is not good. Sudden Infant Death Syndrome (SIDS) is not good. Cancer is not good. Death itself is not good. These things hurt! And Paul understands that and he is not saying that all things are good. Nor is he saying that we will see all of these things working together *now.* The verse simply says that God causes all things to work together.

Now keep in mind, we can't understand this or learn it for the first time in the midst of our pain. This truth has to become real to us *before* we suffer, if it is to carry us through. When we are going through a difficulty, unless this truth has become imbedded in the concrete of our life, the pain can cloud our perspective so that we see only the negative aspects of our experience. One writer puts it so well:

> God, there are times
> In the midst of heartache and heartbreak
> When there is no comfort, no solace
> Anywhere at all.
> There are times
> When in my crumbling state of mind
> I feel I can no longer endure—
> Not for a day, not even an hour.
> It is at such times, O God
> That I draw heavily
> Upon Your unfathomable love.
> At such times I implore
> Your transforming peace.
> At such times I live
> By the power and promises
> Of a Father who cares infinitely more
> Than I can begin to grasp or comprehend.
> Today, dear God, is a "such time."[2]

That can be our perspective, if we grasp the first part of

God's process in trials . . . *He is in control,* but He is also right at hand helping us through, *in all things.*

Now the second aspect of the process is one that we've hinted at already . . . that God works all things together *for good.* No matter what comes, no matter how painful it is, there is an *ultimate* purpose that will be good. Now remember, this verse is not saying that everything will turn out for good in this life. It is not to be seen as grounds for believing that "everything will come out in the wash." The good that Paul mentions is *eternal* good, rather than temporal good. Paul is saying that God causes everything to work out for our *eternal good.*

The word *together* helps us to grasp this emphasis and is crucial to this verse. Paul does not say that God causes individual things, events and circumstances by themselves to work for good, but rather, *all things considered together.* He has a long view in mind.

And that can present a problem for us today because we are so often consumed and concerned only with the present . . . not the future, the now . . . not the then, time . . . not eternity. We struggle with the pieces of our lives that don't seem to fit together; we focus on the immediate, not the ultimate.

Many of us react to life pretty much like a man named Jack. Some time ago, at Mt. Sinai Medical Center in Miami Beach, he had an interesting operation. Jack is five feet, eight inches tall and weighed 300 pounds. He had the upper part of his stomach stapled off so that it can hold only so much food and then he feels full. His plan was to lose 135 pounds through that operation. "That doesn't take much discipline or exercise," you say. That's right—all it took was surgery.

And many of us wish that life was just about that simple . . . we want the staple-gun solutions, the quick answers . . . and we resist the long view, the eternal perspective. And yet that is what Paul has in mind here. Dr. Donald Grey Barnhouse puts it so well in his commentary:

There is no will or act of creatures—men, angels or demons—that can do other than work for our good. No dog can bark against us, no man can speak or act against us, but all must be for our good. There is no phenomenon of nature—fires, flood, storm, earthquake—that can work us ultimate ill. The law of gravity cannot trip us or cause anything to fall upon us unless it has first been sifted through the will of God's purpose for our good. Every experience, each of our individual circumstances . . . whatever concerns us, humbles us and forces us to rely on Him who alone can satisfy. . . . *all things* work together for our (ultimate) good; otherwise the Lord would not permit them.[3]

GOD'S ULTIMATE PURPOSE

Who is in control? Our God is. And because He is in control, He has chosen a process to be used in our lives that includes all things working together, in concert, for our ultimate good. Now we may never be aware of that ultimate good until we see Christ.

But having said that, we need to also say that there is an intended purpose God has in all of our difficulties that we can catch a glimpse of right now. It is described for us in verses 29 and 30.

For whom He foreknew, He also predestined to become conformed to the image of His Son, that He might be the first-born among many brethren; and whom He predestined, these He also called; and whom He called, these He also justified; and whom He justified, these He also glorified.

Now there are several deep, theological terms in these verses, which we could take a long time to explain. You'll be relieved to know that we are not going to do that because, whatever they communicate, they are intended to illustrate that God has been at work in our lives in the past and continues to be at work in our lives for one purpose — that we become "conformed to the image of His Son."

If you are a believer in Jesus Christ, that is God's purpose for you. There are no exceptions. Whatever circumstances you find yourself in, they are all part of God's plan to conform you to Christ. And, by the way, God doesn't waste those conforming experiences.

The word *conformed* was used to describe a coin that was formed, shaped and then imprinted with an image of the emperor. As we are formed and shaped by God in our difficulties, we begin to be imprinted with the image of Christ. And that means that we begin to exhibit changes, that we take on the attitude and perspective of Jesus Christ, especially during painful circumstances.

Jesus Christ suffered greatly in His earthly ministry and He expressed deep anguish and emotion during those times. But He never lost His deep, abiding trust in God the Father's plan and care. That is where we start being conformed to the image of Christ.

But beyond even that, the idea of *conformity* is that God uses suffering in our lives to mature us, to cause us to grow, and that takes *time*. There are no shortcuts to maturity. That is not how God works. His word to us is, "I will mature you and cause you to grow *in My time*, and one of My methods is to weave suffering throughout your life."

What then is the *good* for which all things work together? Can I claim that I'll have a loving husband? Surely that is good. Or children who turn out well? That has got to be good. Or health, a satisfying job, enough money to make me happy? Those things are good, aren't they? That is a human definition of good, but consider God's definition.

The ultimate good — the good that shines above everything else God wants us to have — is explained to us by God Himself in verse 29. Why hadn't I seen it? "For those God foreknew He also predestined to be conformed to the likeness of his Son."

The ultimate good is not happiness in this life, not that souls will rush to know the Savior, not even that finally Christ will be glorified (though these things may result). No. The good that Romans 8:28 is talking about is that we be like Jesus. . . . fashioned in His image . . . conformed to His likeness. To paraphrase it, All things work together for the ultimate good purpose of making us like Jesus.[4]

My friends, believe it or not, that is what happens during trials. You are focusing on the chips, God is focusing on the image. You're looking at what you call lost from your perspective, but it is the very thing which God calls valuable from His.

WITHIN GOD'S KEEPING

Now, having said all that, let me make two brief and final observations from verse 28. The first is that this text is for Christians only. The assurance of these verses is not applicable to everyone who suffers. Paul confines the relevance of this great hope to "those who love God, those who are called according to His purpose." In fact, in the original text, the words "and we know that those who love God," stand at the very beginning of the sentence. And the intent, then, is that they, and they alone, have a right to be comforted by this text. Only for those who love God — those who have come into a personal relationship with Jesus Christ by faith — is it true that God causes all things to work together for good. If you are not a believer in Jesus Christ, this is not for you. It is not supposed to be. It was that knowledge that pushed Somerset Maugham to write, "It is not true that suffering ennobles the character; happiness does that sometimes, but suffering for the most part makes men petty and vindictive."[5]

And that brings us to the second and final observation. If

you are a believer in Jesus Christ then you need to wrap
your soul in these verses, because Paul assures us that this
promise is for us when he writes in verse 28, *"And we
know."* It does not say, "And we feel, we hope, we pray, we
imagine, we desire, we guess, we'd like." It says, *we know.*
And the word means "we have an absolute, unshakeable
knowledge" that this is true.

> Significantly, Paul and the people to whom he was
> writing were living through a time of great injustice
> and political tyranny. Many died as innocent victims.
> Far from being clear that they would be winners when
> history tabulated the results, it seemed Christ's follow-
> ers were actually victims being crushed by forces of
> imperial power, social intolerance, and indiscriminate
> evil. Moreover, they lived in a time of ravaging illness
> without anesthetics or antiseptics. His text within this
> context is either pretext or a pledge of a wonderful
> source of consolation.[6]

I'll vote for the second option. How about you?

In 1895, Andrew Murray was in England suffering from
a terribly painful back, the result of an injury he had in-
curred years before. One morning while he was eating
breakfast in his room, his hostess told him of a woman
downstairs who was in great trouble and wanted to know if
he had any advice for her. Andrew Murray handed her a
paper he had been writing on and said, "Give her this
advice I'm writing down for myself. It may be that she'll
find it helpful." This is what was written and it says it all.

> In time of trouble, say, "First, He brought me here. It
> is by His will I am in this strait place, in that I will
> rest." Next, "He will keep me here in His love, and
> give me grace in this trial to behave as His child."
> Then say, "He will make the trial a blessing, teaching
> me lessons He intends me to learn, and working in the
> grace He means to bestow." And last, say, "In His
> good time He can bring me out again. How and when,
> He knows." Therefore, say, "I am here (1) by God's

appointment, (2) in His keeping, (3) under His training, (4) for His time."[7]

When the pebbles bounce off the freeway of your life
and crack the crystal-clear window of your circumstances,
keep watching and looking. God is still there and He loves
you deeply. You'll find Him, believe me, even in the
dark . . . just keep looking for His light.

Notes

C H A P T E R   O N E

1. Max Lucado, *In the Eye of the Storm* (Dallas: Word, Inc., 1991), 105–6.
2. Cited by D. Edmond Hiebert, *First Peter: An Expositional Commentary* (Chicago: Moody Press, 1984), 268.
3. Malcolm Muggeridge, *A Twentieth Century Testimony* (Nashville: Thomas Nelson, 1978), 35.
4. Ruth Harms Calkin, *Lord, Don't You Love Me Anymore?* (Wheaton, Ill.: Tyndale House Publishers, 1988), 71.
5. Dietrich Bonhoeffer, *The Cost of Discipleship* (New York: Macmillan Publishing Company, 1963), 100–101.
6. Tim Hansel, *You Gotta Keep Dancin'* (Elgin, Ill.; David C. Cook Publishing Co., 1985), 55.
7. Calkin, Ibid., 61.
8. Adapted from Kenneth W. Osbeck *101 Hymn Stories*, (Grand Rapids: Kregel Publications, 1982), 57–59.
9. Wayne Grudem, *First Peter* (Grand Rapids: Wm. B. Eerdmans Publishing Company, 1989), 184–85.

C H A P T E R   T W O

1. Clayton and Peggy Bell, "A Look at Grief," *Leadership,* Fall 1980, Vol. 1. Number 4, 40.
2. Cited by Warren Wiersbe, "Playing David's Harp," in *Propkope,* Nov./Dec. 1986, Vol. III, No. 6, (Lincoln, Neb. 68501), 1.
3. H.C. Leopold, *Exposition of the Psalms* (Grand Rapids: Baker Book House, 1969), 67.
4. Chuck Swindoll, *Home, Where Life Makes Up Its Mind* (Portland: Multnomah Press, 1979), 98–99.
5. Anonymous, cited by Ted W. Engstrom and Robert C. Larson in *Integrity* (Waco, Texas: Word, Inc., 1987), 87.
6. E.M. Blaiklock, *Commentary on the Psalms*, Vol. 1 (Philadelphia: A.J. Holman Co., 1977), 15.
7. Willard Gaylin, *The Rage Within: Anger in Modern Life*, (New York: Simon and Schuster, 1984), 33.
8. Lois Johnson (source unknown)
9. Cited by Gail MacDonald in *High Call, High Privilege*, (Wheaton, Ill.:

Tyndale House Publishers, Inc., 1981), 34–35.

10. G. Campbell Morgan, *The Westminister Pulpit*, Vol. IV (Grand Rapids: Baker Book House, 1954–1955), 49.

11. J.I. Packer, *Hot Tub Religion* (Wheaton, Ill.: Tyndale House Publishers, Inc., 1987), 73.

12. Lloyd John Ogilvie, *Drumbeat of Love* (Waco, Texas: Word, Inc., 1976), 176.

13. John Calvin, cited by W.S Plumer in *Psalms* (Carlisle, Pa.: The Banner of Truth Trust, 1975), 72.

CHAPTER THREE

1. Ben Haden. From his radio program "Changed Lives." Used by permission.

2. Edith Schaeffer, *Affliction* (Old Tappan, N.J.: Fleming H. Revell Company, 1978), 13.

3. Cited by Batsell B. Baxter, *When Life Tumbles In* (Grand Rapids: Baker Book House, 1974), 23.

4. Thomas Wolfe, *The Anatomy of Loneliness* cited by George Seldes in "The Great Thoughts" (New York: Ballantine Books, 1985), 457.

5. Alec Motyer, *The Message of James* (Downers Grove, Ill.: InterVarsity Press, 1985), 30.

6. *U.S. News and World Report*, 13 July, 1987, 13.

7. Eugene Peterson, *A Long Obedience in the Same Direction* (Downers Grove, Ill.: InterVarsity Press, 1985), 30.

8. Marilyn Meberg, *Choosing the Amusing* (Portland: Multnomah Press, 1986) 129–30.

9. Source unknown.

10. C.S. Lewis, *A Grief Observed* (New York: The Seabury Press, 1961), 9.

11. Alan Redpath, *Victorious Christian Living* (Old Tappan, N.J.: Fleming H. Revell Company, 1955), 166.

CHAPTER FOUR

1. Charles R. Swindoll, *Home, Where Life Makes Up Its Mind* (Portland: Multnomah Press, 1979), 47–48.

2. Philip Yancey, *Disappointment With God* (Grand Rapids: Zondervan Publishing House, 1988), 23.

3. Margaret Clarkson in *The Banner*, 19 Nov. 1984, cited in *Christianity Today*, 9 Dec. 1988, 34.

4. Joseph Bayly, *Psalms of My Life* (Elgin, Ill.: David C. Cook Publishing Company, 1987), 25.

5. Author unknown.

6. Charles Colson, *Who Speaks for God?* (Westchester, Ill.: Crossway Books, 1985), 62–63.

7. Harold Myra, *Living by God's Surprises*, 84, cited in *The Pastor's Story File*, Vol. 4, #10, August 1988.
8. William Temple, *Reading in St. John's Gospel* first ser. (London: Macmillan, 1939), 68.

CHAPTER FIVE

1. Ben Haden. From his radio program "Changed Lives." Used by permission.
2. T.S. Eliot, *Murder in the Cathedral*, cited in *Leadership*, Spring 1987, "When Will Our Tears Cease?" 20.
3. Willard Gaylin, *The Rage Within: Anger in Modern Life* (New York: Simon and Schuster, 1984), 24.
4. Source unknown.
5. Richard C. Halverson, *No Greater Power* (Portland: Multnomah Press, 1986), 51.
6. Alan Paton, "Meditation of a Young Boy Confirmed," quoted by Robert Raines in *Creative Brooding* (New York: Macmillan Company, 1968), 20.
7. J.I. Packer, *Knowing God* (Downers Grove, Ill.: InterVarsity Press, 1979), 181–82.
8. Ruth Harms Calkin, *Tell Me Again, Lord, I Forget* (Wheaton, Ill.: Tyndale House Publishers, 1974), 83.
9. Max Lucado, *God Came Near* (Portland: Multnomah Press, 1987), 124–25.

CHAPTER SIX

1. Robin and John Drakeford, *In Praise of Women* (San Francisco, Harper & Row, 1980), 103.
2. Alexander Maclaren, *The Psalms* in the *Expositor's Bible*, Vol. III (Grand Rapids: Baker Book House, 1982), 145–46.
3. David Augsburger, *When Enough Is Enough* (Ventura, Calif.: Regal Books, 1984), 11.
4. H. Norman Wright, *Making Peace With Your Past* (Old Tappan, N.J.: Fleming H. Revell Company, 1985), 65.
5. Lewis B. Smedes, *Caring and Commitment* (San Francisco: Harper and Row Publishers, 1988), 120–21.
6. Alexander Maclaren, loc. cit.
7. Philip G. Zimbardo, "The Age of Indifference," in *Psychology Today*, August 1980, 72.
8. Hannah Whitehall Smith, *The Christian's Secret of a Happy Life*, cited by *Christianity Today*, March 1987, 41.
9. Cited in *Parables, Etc.*, January 1986, 7.
10. Peter Marshall, source unknown.

CHAPTER SEVEN

1. Max Lucado, *Six Hours One Friday* (Portland: Multnomah Press: 1989), 35–38.
2. Joseph Parker, *The People's Bible*, Vol. XII, (London: Hazell, Watson and Viney, LD, 1898), 249–50.
3. Cited by James C. Dobson, *Love Must Be Tough* (Waco, Texas: Word, Inc., 1984), 208–9.
4. Joyce Landorf, *Change Points* (Old Tappan, N.J.: Fleming H. Revell, 1981), 105.
5. "Stress: Can We Cope?" *Time*, 6 June 1983, 48–54.
6. *Preaching*, January–February 1987, Vol. 11, Number 4, 53.
7. David Dickson, *A Commentary on the Psalms* (Carlisle, Pa.: The Banner of Truth Trust, 1985), 412.
8. Cited by Michael P. Green, editor, *Illustrations for Biblical Preaching* (Grand Rapids: Baker Book House, 1989), 183.
9. H. Norman Wright, *Seasons of a Marriage*, (Ventura, Calif.: Regal, 1982), 137–38.
10. Alexander Maclaren, *The Epistles of St. Paul to the Colossians and Philemon* in the *Expositor's Bible*, Vol. VI, (Grand Rapids: Baker Book House, 1982), 235.

CHAPTER EIGHT

1. Ben Haden. From his radio program "Changed Lives." Used by permission.
2. M. Scott Peck, *The Road Less Traveled* (New York: Simon and Schuster, 1978), 16–17.
3. Homer A. Kent, *Faith That Works* (Grand Rapids: Baker Book House, 1986), 39.
4. Douglas J. Moo, *James*, in the *Tyndale New Testament Commentaries* (Grand Rapids: Wm. B. Eerdmans Publishing Company, 1986), 65.
5. "Either One," from *Jesus Makes the Difference*, by James A. Harnish, cited in *Parables, Etc.*, August 1987, 1.
6. Richard C. Halverson, *No Greater Power* (Portland: Multnomah Press, 1986), 198–99.
7. A.W. Tozer, *The Root of the Righteous* (Harrisburg, Pa.: Christian Publications, Inc., 1955), 50.
8. Alec Motyer, *The Message of James* (Downers Grove, Ill.: InterVarsity Press, 1985), 44.
9. Willard Gaylin, *The Rage Within: Anger in Modern Life* (New York: Simon and Schuster, 1984), 145.
10. Michael P. Green, editor, *Illustrations for Biblical Preaching* (Grand Rapids: Baker Book House, 1989), 249.
11. Judith M. Bardwick, *The Plateauing Trap* (New York: American Management Association, 1986), 13.

C H A P T E R   N I N E

1. Ben Haden. From his radio program, "Changed Lives." Used by permission.
2. *International Children's Bible* (Waco, Texas: Word, Inc., 1986).
3. Gail and Gordon MacDonald, *If Those Who Reach Could Touch* (Old Tappan, N.J.: Fleming H. Revell Company, 1984), 92.
4. Joseph Bayly, *Psalms of My Life* (Elgin, Ill.: David C. Cook Publishing Co., 1987), 17.
5. J.I. Packer, *Hot Tub Religion* (Wheaton, Ill.: Tyndale House Publishers, Inc., 1987), 80–81.
6. Bill Butterworth, *My Kids Are My Best Teachers* (Old Tappan, N.J.: Fleming H. Revell Company, 1986), 93–94.
7. Scott Peck, *The Road Less Traveled* (New York: Simon and Schuster, 1978), 15.
8. John Blanchard, *Truth for Life, A Devotional Commentary on the Epistle of James* (Welwyn Hertfordshire, England: Evangelical Press, 1986), 344.
9. Charles R. Swindoll, *Strengthening Your Grip* (Waco, Texas: Word, Inc., 1982), 213.
10. Cited by Gary Inrig, *A Call to Excellence* (Wheaton, Ill.: Victor Books, 1985), 111.
11. Maxie Dunnam, "I Am the Door" (*Preaching Today*, Tape #53)

C H A P T E R   T E N

1. Michael P. Green, editor, *Illustrations for Biblical Preaching* (Grand Rapids: Baker Book House, 1989), 365–66.
2. Ibid., 383–84.
3. M. Scott Peck, *The Road Less Traveled* (New York: Simon and Schuster, 1978), 15.
4. Max Lucado, *On the Anvil,* (Wheaton, Ill.: Tyndale House Publishers, 1985), 11–12.
5. Ruth Harms Calkin, *Lord, Don't You Love Me Anymore?* (Wheaton, Ill.: Tyndale House Publishers, 1988), 49.
6. Ben Haden. From his radio program, "Changed Lives." Used by permission.
7. A.W. Tozer, *The Root of the Righteous* (Harrisburg, Pa: Christian Publications, Inc., 1955), 50.
8. Edmond P. Clowney, *The Message of First Peter* (Downers Grove, Ill.: InterVarsity Press, 1988), 58.

C H A P T E R   E L E V E N

1. Edith Schaeffer, *Affliction* (Old Tappan, N.J.: Fleming H. Revell Company, 1978), 13–14.

2. Ruth Harms Calkin, *Lord, Don't You Love Me Anymore?* (Wheaton, Ill.: Tyndale House Publishers, 1988), 35.

3. Donald Grey Barnhouse, *Romans, God's Grace, God's Freedom, God's Heirs* (Grand Rapids: Wm. B. Eerdmans Publishing Company, 1982), 158.

4. Carole Mayhall, *Help, Lord, My Whole Life Hurts* (Colorado Springs: NavPress, 1988), 153–54.

5. W.S. Maugham: *The Moon and Sixpence,* cited by Bergen Evans, *Dictionary of Quotations,* (New York: Bonanza Books, 1968), 667.

6. Robert Wise, *When the Night Is Too Long* (Nashville: Thomas Nelson, 1990), 23.

7. James C. Hefley, *A Dictionary of Illustrations* (Grand Rapids: Zondervan Publishing House, 1971), 297.

Acknowledgments

The following publishers have given permission for their works to be reproduced in this book:

"Broken Hearted Me" (Randy Goodrum) © 1979 Chappell & Co. & Sailmaker Music. All rights administered by Chappell & Co. All rights reserved. Used by permission.

Psalms of My Life by Joe Bayly. Used with permission by David C. Cook Publishing Co. © 1987, available at your local Christian bookstore.

On the Anvil, pp. 11–12, by Max Lucado © 1985. Used by permission of Tyndale House Publishers, Inc. All rights reserved.

Lord, Don't You Love Me Anymore? by Ruth Harms Calkin, © 1988. Used by permission of Tyndale House Publishers, Inc. All rights reserved.

Tell Me Again Lord, I Forget, by Ruth Harms Calkin, © 1974. Used by permission of Tyndale House Publishers, Inc. All rights reserved.

In the Eye of the Storm, Max Lucado, © 1981, Word, Inc., Dallas, Texas. Used by permission.

Living by God's Surprises, Harold Myra, © 1988, Word, Inc. Dallas, Texas. Used with permission.

Drumbeat of Love, Dr. Lloyd John Ogilvie, © 1979, Word, Inc., Dallas, Texas. Used with permission.